A Self Help Handbook

# BE THE VOICE
## YOU CAN'T CHANGE THE PAST, ONLY HOW YOU RESPOND TO IT

by George Lee Sye

**SOARENT PUBLISHING**

PO Box 267, Ravenshoe, Queensland, AUSTRALIA 4888

georgeleesye.com/books

© 2025-2026 by George Lee Sye - All Rights Reserved

(Printed Version) ISBN: 978-0-6457182-1-8
(eBook Version) ISBN: 978-0-6457182-2-5

# NOTES

# CONTENTS

**A Mountain of Voices** ................................................................... 5
**Preface** ........................................................................................... 8
    A Life Changing Phone Call ...................................................... 8
    The Early Years ......................................................................... 11
    Be The Voice ............................................................................. 13
    The Question is the Answer ..................................................... 14
    Special Questions in Special Operations ................................. 16
    This Book .................................................................................. 23
**Controlling The Voice Inside** .................................................... 25
    Mind Experiments ..................................................................... 25
    What Do Questions Really Do? ................................................ 26
    Learned Patterns of Thinking ................................................... 28
    Questions Are The Key ............................................................. 34
    The Importance of Emotional State .......................................... 37
    Six Achievable Outcomes ......................................................... 38
    Four Types of Questions ........................................................... 54
    1. Changing How We Feel About Experiences ........................ 54
    2. Focusing On Solutions and Options ..................................... 69
    3. Taking Action ....................................................................... 69
    4. Taking Responsibility .......................................................... 71
**Final Thoughts** ............................................................................ 74
    The Resources Are There Already ........................................... 75
    The First Responder Paradox ................................................... 76
    You Have A Choice .................................................................. 77
    Man's Search for Meaning ....................................................... 78
**Appendices** .................................................................................. 80
    A: Revisiting Past Tragedies, When You Should and Shouldn't .............. 80
    B: Question Based Conversational Tools ................................. 83

About the Author ........................................................................................103
Acknowledgements ....................................................................................105
Companion Read: Problem Warrior..........................................................106

# A Mountain of Voices

We'd only shut our eyes for what seemed like a minute. It was around 2:00 am when the dreaded "get your asses out of bed" call erupted through the shed, shattering the peace of some well deserved shut eye.

A rag tag bunch of weary men, now some 48 hours into a long and testing 72 hour pre-selection program, had stayed dressed for the anticipated call out. The men sat up, almost in unison, and put their running shoes on.

They all knew that this morning's task was going to be another one of the special emergency response team's activities designed to test their metal to the core.

We all bundled into the back of the vehicles, not wanting to be last in case that led to some surprising punishment. As we made our way to some unknown location, I rocked with the movement of the land cruiser and closed my eyes. I let the weariness take over and quietly dozed in my little corner of the vehicle. It was these moments that seemed to refuel me, they were a part of my strategy for getting through this.

I thought it interesting that when we got back to the base camp after each punishing activity, most other candidates would go straight to their stretchers, lay down and get some sleep.

My approach was different. I would get back to the base camp and the first thing I did was dry my feet, put powder on them to help with that, and hydrate my body. The goal was to ensure the two things that would stop me from completing this were looked after. If I didn't get any sleep so be it. I knew that we were always going to be transported somewhere by vehicle for every activity, so those were the times I would get my chance to catch up on a little sleep with a power nap. Amazingly it worked, for me anyway.

It was dark and quiet when we stopped somewhere at the bottom of Mount Coot-tha on the outskirts of Brisbane.

## BE THE VOICE

Mount Coot-tha is a prominent natural landmark located just west of Brisbane's city centre in Queensland, Australia. Rising to approximately 287 metres above sea level, it forms part of the D'Aguilar Range and offers expansive views of the city skyline, Moreton Bay, and beyond. Renowned for its lush bushland, winding trails, and rugged terrain, Mount Coot-tha is a popular destination for hikers, cyclists, and those seeking physical challenge and natural beauty close to the urban heart of Brisbane.

This mountain is more than just a scenic escape—it is also a proving ground. Its steep ascents, dense forest paths, and unpredictable weather conditions have made it a favoured training location.

The Sir Samuel Griffith Drive forms a loop around Mount Coot-tha. This scenic drive is approximately 10 to 11 kilometres long and offers panoramic views of Brisbane and its surroundings. It's a popular route for motorists and cyclists alike.

Our task this morning was to complete what was to become in future years a notorious group activity requiring us to carrying an extremely heavy log up and around the mountain circuit that followed Sir Samuel Griffith Drive.

The first thing I noticed about the log was that it was actually an old used power pole. The most awkward thing about it was it had three metal spikes, about 10 mm in diameter, sticking out of it. Two were at one end of the log, and one stuck out at the other end.

Talk about difficult to carry, just trying to hang on to the log was a nightmare. Three of the team were able to use the spikes, everyone else had to do the best they could to support the weight of the log.

I remember jogging slowly along hanging on to one of the spikes when it was my turn. The physical pain those spikes caused forced me to draw on every bit of self control I had, just to keep going and not complain.

We'd stop and rotate frequently, someone else would take hold of the spike while I moved to a position beside the main body of the log.

## BE THE VOICE

Hooking the crook of arm underneath the log seemed to be the best way to hold at least some part of the weight. But jogging and walking at the same time, all while instructors were screaming at us, was very challenging.

There were moments when that voice in my brain would come up with excuses that would justify stopping. "Tell them your knee has failed." "Your carrying an old injury that prevents you from doing this."

It was all bullshit. I wanted to complete this, and that voice was from someone who didn't. I knew that. I remember looking at one of the instructors and smiling. I repeated one thought quietly to myself; "there is nothing you pussies can do to me that will make me stop."

Some candidates didn't make it, they withdrew. I didn't. Then and now, I choose to be the voice that controls the conversation in my head.

# Preface

## A Life Changing Phone Call

I got the phone call late at night, around 11:00 pm from memory.

"I can't find your dad, he just left and I'm worried about him."

Daphne's voice conveyed her deep concern for the welfare of my father who had been with her some hours before.

Strangely, I immediately experienced this strong feeling of dread. I had no real reason for that, it was a gut feel.

"I'll go look for him" I told her. I jumped in my car and drove out, not really sure of where I'd even start to look. I took a drive past a couple of houses that I knew belonged to friends of his but there was no sign of his Toyota van.

What was even stranger, was the nagging feeling I had about where he might have gone.

Wind back the clock about 4 hours. Myself and Vicki had gone over to where dad was staying with Daphne. My young half brother Mark, and half sister Sam, children of dad's from his second marriage, were both there too. This was planned to be a small family gathering to wrap up the year (1981) and celebrate new years eve.

I believe dad and Daphne were going to head south again to return to the small property dad had purchased in Tasmania, and this was the last chance we had to get together.

Everything seemed quite normal. Dad had separated from his second wife some six months earlier and it seemed like things had settled. He had hinted that it was tough being away from the kids, but in spite of that, it appeared as though he had moved on in some positive way. He and

## BE THE VOICE

Daphne were happy together, and photos of them on the Tasmanian property seems to support this.

We ended the night with hugs all round, smiles and laughter. Little did I know it would be the last time I saw my father alive.

With the help of dad a few months earlier, I'd set up a small motor mechanic's workshop in one of the back suburbs of Cairns. The workshop was located in a multi shed complex, I think there might have been around eight sheds in total.

It was nothing fancy, just a collection of small lockable areas with a single small window and a roller door on the front of each, and space for maybe three cars inside at most.

The driveway in the complex ran between the sheds connecting one street to another. Half of them faced the driveway from one side and half faced the driveway on the other side.

For some very strange reason I had this urge to look for dad over at my workshop. It might have been around midnight or even a little later whenI drove into the complex and stopped the car in the middle of the centre driveway. I turned it off and as I stepped out, I could hear the sound of an engine running.

I knew, I just knew exactly what I was going to find. I ran to the shed where the noise was coming from and looked through the small window on the front.

Inside I could see dad's green Toyota van parked backwards with the front facing the roller door. It had been reversed into the shed. The engine was running and I noticed a warmth on the glass of the window that should not have been there.

I back away from the window towards the area in front and then shoulder charged the left side of the roller door. The door bulged inwards and pulled out of the runners on one side, creating a space I could climb through and get into the shed.

Dad looked like he'd simply gone to sleep. The sliding side door of the van was open, and dad was laying back with his head tilted towards the open door. It seem obvious to me that he had coughed as his false teeth were partially out of his mouth. I grabbed him by the arm and realised he felt very warm and strangely quite rigid. I felt for a pulse but it wasn't there. The knowledge that dad was no longer with us and nothing could be done hit me like a sledgehammer in the chest.

The gases inside the shed were terrible, they burnt my throat and it took weeks for the inevitable coughing to go away. But the lasting part that will never go away are the images I have of finding my dad after he had committed suicide.

That event had an enormous impact on not only me, but also the other kids.

Sam continued to live with her mother. Mark was obviously having difficulties, so he moved in with Vicki and I for a while. I got him involved in motorcycle riding and camping, and I actually thought he was doing well. I never knew how deep his wounds actually were. Mark ended up taking his own life. He had tried multiple times to commit suicide and eventually succeeded by jumping off a major bridge structure.

In late 2008 my sister Karen, who had been suffering from serious mental problems including diagnosed schizophrenia, disappeared not far from my current home up in the mountains. Suicide was suspected but I guess we'll never know. To date she has not been found.

What many people don't know is that my father's dad also took his own life when dad was quite young. He turned up one day at dad's school, and basically said good bye. He then left and that same day drank poison and died a horrible death. Everything pointed towards this all being related to a breakdown of his relationship with a woman.

Geezus, I sit here and shake my head as I write this. What is this run of suicides in my family? Do we have some genetic disposition to ending our own lives when things get hard?

Like all small to medium enterprises, we've had some highs and lows over the past 25 years in running our business. Personally, I am still reeling from the financial impacts of the government shutting us down for more than a year as part of its disastrous and ill-thought out COVID pandemic response. Just one more challenge to deal with.

Unfortunately, my closest friends and some family are aware of the pressures, as well as my family history. So even as recent as this year (2025), people worry about me being suicidal.

Well, fortunately, nothing could be further from the truth.

# The Early Years

My life has been pretty remarkable. I roll over 66 years in a couple of months [at the time of writing this]. I have my health, probably way better than most people my age. I have the energy levels of a much younger dude, and can still do things that many my age can't or won't do.

But those 66 years have not been without their challenges.

When I was 9 years old, I would spend time at a youth club in Sydney where we lived at the time. One of the club gymnastics coaches would take me into the men's showers with him at the end of each attendance. That was a scary time. There was nobody to talk to back then, I was so frightened by it I felt I couldn't tell anyone, even my mother who I lived with. In fact I still haven't told her. Every time I got dropped off at the youth club I walked in with feelings of dread. It affected by ability to do the gymnastics, every time I went there the attention from that man was really upsetting, but there was nothing I could do about it.

## BE THE VOICE

Eventually we moved north to Cairns after mum met Jim, the first of my step fathers. I felt much safer and had a great time attending the final years of primary school.

Right on the change over to high school, we moved to Townsville where Jim took up a new job in sales, and I started the first of my three years in high school.

Some months into our move there, a man who had befriended my mother and step father, I can't remember his name only his face, started coming into my room at night after I'd gone to bed. It scared me. The same thing was happening again, and this time in my own home. I never understood how that could happen with both my mother and step father at home.

The situation came to a head when I found this man with my sister. They had made a tent on the back porch with a couple of sheets. I had peeked into the tent through a gap and saw this bloke doing things he should not have been doing, so I told mum what I'd seen.

She, or it might have been my step father, immediately reported him to police. He was arrested, charged, convicted and sent to jail. I never spoke to the police during that investigation, and nobody ever asked me about any dealings he'd had with me.

Those two events had an affect on me that I had to work around for a very long time. People I worked with probably never knew about the fear and anxiety I was dealing with when talking or presenting to men specifically who held positions of authority. It was strange that I knew these men could not compete with me physically, yet I was incredibly intimidated by being in their presence. I never really escaped those feelings until I was around 50 years of age. I believe it was my continual persistence to do those presentations, regardless of the emotions I felt, that eventually resolved it.

As a police officer from the early 80s to late 90s I was involved in many incidents involved death and injury. I attended numerous fatal car and motorcycle accidents, responded to suicides, and was first responder to murders and shootings.

I also attended aircraft crash scenes, four to be precise. One was as the senior officer charged with locating the aircraft and coordinating the recovery. The task at the other three involved removing the bodies of the victims. One time I had to cut off the legs of a deceased person with a pocket knife in order to retrieve his body from a crushed helicopter wreckage. That action was necessary as the crash had taken place in an extremely difficult location to get to on the steepest and most inaccessible side of a mountain.

I tell you this for no other reason than to simply highlight that there have been some quite significant challenges and emotional events take place in my life, just as you've been confronted with challenges and events in your life.

Yet I feel I've been able to get to this point in my life in a way that has been empowering. The main factors that contributed to that are these:

1. Acknowledging that I need challenge in my life in order to grow,

2. Recognising that I really appreciate the sunny day only because there have been rainy days, and

3. Taking charge of that voice inside my head.

# Be The Voice

I learnt a long time ago that I had a choice. I could focus on all of the negative aspects of everything that has happened to me and around me. I could replay those images of finding dad and take the 'why me' route of self pity.

I could think about my brother Mark and how I tried and failed to help him straighten out his life and focus on the negativity of it all.

I could ponder how unsuccessful I had been in helping my sister with her problems. It's true, I tried and failed there too.

I could continually playback the details of all of the tragedies and emotions that have taken place.

Or was it possible that I could choose a different pathway?

It seemed to me that I did have a choice of options here. I also had the option to get control of my own response to all of those events by taking control of the conversations I had with myself.

It was this understanding that I could either let the voice in my head run rampant, or proactively be that voice and take control of the questions and answers I gave myself.

I chose to be the voice. I made the decision a long time ago to turn the negative events of my life into meaningful lessons that made me stronger and wiser than I would have otherwise been.

That's what this book is about, proactively being the voice inside your head. I know deep in my heart that this will surely help others.

# The Question is the Answer

Some years ago I took a trip to Perth in Western Australia where I noticed a poster in a bookshop display window advertising Dan Brown's book, 'The da Vinci Code'.

What intrigued me was not the picture on it, the Mona Lisa painting, but rather the question that accompanied it.

BE THE VOICE

That's definitely not a misprint; that is the *actual* question that appeared on the poster.

I've probably seen the Mona Lisa a hundred times, yet this question radically changed how I looked at the picture. The conversation in my head was altered, as was my mental focus and how I perceived that picture, all because of one simple question.

That brain of yours might just be the most sophisticated computer on the planet. I think you know that already. The only problem for us is that it doesn't come with a handbook on how to use the thing.

Our conscious and unconscious thinking patterns are the starting point for our emotions. What we perceive and how our brain responds causes us to experience feelings. And it's these emotions that drive our behaviour.

So it makes sense to me that if we can get control of our thinking patterns, we should be able to control our feelings and behaviours more effectively than if we let them run rampant and uncontrolled.

The brain doesn't know right from wrong. It knows only where it's focused. For example, the golfer standing on the tee is the one who consciously decides to look at and give attention to the water hazard in front of them, it is they who plays back the memory of the last time they stood here and smacked it right into the drink, it is they who decides that water is bad. Unfortunately the subconscious part of the brain of that golfer only knows it is focusing on the water. The feelings that come from that focus inevitably lead to it all being reinforced when the ball flies so elegantly to leave its rippled sign of entry smack bang in the middle of the lake.

You might have heard it said that it's better to say to a child "hold the scissors firmly" rather than say "don't drop the scissors". It's the same thing, one causes the brain to focus on holding it, the other focuses the brain on dropping it.

To find out how to get control of the brain we have to discover how to direct its focus. And that's where internal conversations and specifically questions come into play. They constitute the vehicle for controlling the conversation and focus of our minds.

The conversations you have inside your head and the questions you ask yourself have a tremendous impact on your life. They can empower you for sure, or they can disempower you. They can cause you to find answers for how to change any situation, or they can hold you back from doing anything.

The ability to ask great questions, not just of others but of yourself, is one of the most profound yet simple skills you can ever learn. And it is a skill that can rapidly enhance your performance as a parent, a partner, a friend, a manager of people, or even as a leader.

# Special Questions in Special Operations

The art of questioning has intrigued me for many years, particularly during the time when I performed special operations in government service. In a ten year period, I was involved in four hundred and ten jobs, many of which are fascinating stories in their own right.

The Author Running Special Operations Training

I cast my mind back to a particular operation conducted in the northern part of Australia during the 1990s. The work was conducted over almost three months and involved the location of an enormous drug operation which had been sighted by a special form of aerial surveillance.

New surveillance technology was involved and the information was presented to us to see if it was useful in the detection and prosecution of offenders involved in these types of activities. The location of the operation had been plotted on a map and given directly to our unit. However, a fundamental error had been made. The site had been originally plotted by a third party with the information analysed upside down. As a result the actual area was some 20 to 30 kilometres to the north-west of where we thought it would be.

The first trip we made into the field was based on this erroneous mapping of the location. Five team members and I spent 72 hours searching and covering quite mountainous terrain, all to no avail. We did find a water hole with the most dense population of Barramundi fish I have ever seen in one location, but no drug site.

I still kick myself today to think I never threw a line into that water hole. And do you think I can remember now where it was? Of course not.

No matter. When we finally returned to our pick up rendezvous, we had covered more than 50 kilometres on foot. It was a great workout and all of us trimmed down to the tune of a few kilograms, but we didn't produce the result expected.

We went back to the drawing board. We eventually worked out that the location had been wrongly plotted on the map and corrected it. Because the terrain involved was so dense and mountainous, and the size of the area was so large, we decided that a surveillance operation would be the most appropriate, so began one of the more time consuming operations I'd been involved in.

Over the period of the next three months, we sent my team and teams from other units into the field and rotated about every seven to fourteen days.

A number of minor sightings of vehicles as well as a sighting of a helicopter helped us narrow down the target area to the north west of where we had originally started our search.

Into the third month, the teams from our unit had positioned the main surveillance point near an intersection of dirt tracks opposite a small farm house.

Each team would be dropped off at around 2:00 am and then travel some 10 kilometres on foot for a changeover with the outgoing team. They would remain in place for up to a fortnight before being replaced by another team. The teams in the field had support crews located some 30 kilometres away with whom they would communicate on a regular prearranged basis. Support crews would also undertake a rostered rotation.

## BE THE VOICE

I vividly remember the last two weeks of the operation. Before going back into the field with my team, I had been called to a meeting with my boss and the Chief Superintendent of the region who wanted to know what we believed we could achieve. The operation had been going for almost three months and was tying up valuable resources from a number of key operational areas. It was costing a lot of money and senior people were getting quite edgy about the whole operation.

"What do you believe George?" he asked.

"I believed we can locate the site Sir. If we have no sighting in the next week, we will make a foot search of the area. Give us two more weeks." I told him.

Based on his faith in what we could do, he went with that decision and really put his reputation and my boss's reputation on the line.

At about 2:00 am, three other team members and I were dropped off at the planned point.

We then spent the next three to four hours walking into the surveillance location where we did our changeover with an incredibly smelly bunch of bearded guys who'd come up from Townsville and had just had a two week vacation in the bush. Well that's what I told them it was.

The next morning we restarted the routine. The guys would secrete themselves into 'hides' during the dark of the morning. They would spend the day observing in a particular direction before being extracted at night. We would spend each night in our hootchies in a well hidden base camp some two kilometres from the surveillance point.

On about the fourth day we got a break. Two of the team noticed a motor bike being ridden into the intersection before stopping at the closed gate. The rider got off, opened the gate, pushed the bike through and then wiped his wheel tracks with the leaves of a large tree branch that was lying on the side of the road. He then closed the gate and rode away.

*A Team Member Surveilling From A Tall Tree*

We decided to attempt tracking the bike, believing that it was associated with the drug operation. So two other team members and I packed enough equipment and supplies for about four days.

We left one member at the base surveillance site, and we then began the task of following the track from the point where the bike had last been seen. We each carried about 30 to 35 kilograms of food and equipment so the movement was slow and deliberate.

As we moved in, we noticed that the bike had been ridden off to the side, avoiding the dirt track itself. As you can imagine, following the track was at times quite difficult. Over the next two days we walked quite a long way, travelling slowly and, on many occasions, back tracking to try to find sign of the bike.

On the morning of the third day we located the motor bike. It had been concealed in a small depression and was lying on its side covered with branches and foliage. Someone walking within five metres of it could easily have walked straight past without noticing it.

It was at that point I believed we were close to the site and that the task would be easy to wrap up. Well how wrong was I?

Up until that time we had been tracking a motor cycle which left quite a distinct mark. The difficulty now was that we were no longer following a heavy piece of machinery, but a person on foot with the intent of concealing his or her tracks. If it was slow and tedious before, we knew it was going to be even slower from now on.

We started by moving in what seemed to be the obvious direction from the bike's location, and then moving in arcs back and forth until we found some sign of movement on foot by a person. The work was painstaking and on many occasions we had to go back to the last sighting and start again.

Over the course of the next four or five hours it seemed that we were not going to find where the rider had walked. The track just seemed to disappear. We must have started the whole process again from the bike's location on at least six occasions. We had scouted around in ever increasing circles but it seemed that the rider had simply vanished. By mid-afternoon we were just about spent. I remember the three of us sitting in a dried up creek bed, having a drink and eating a snack. Even the opportunity to eat one of our squashed and hot muesli bars which we had grown to love [he says with a facetious tone] had lost its appeal.

One of the guys openly communicated his thoughts. "This is a waste of our time, there's no point going on."

I had been in the unit close to ten years and if there was one thing I had learnt about keeping these guys moving was to the need keep them focused on the outcome. The best way I had found to do that was to ask the right questions. At this point we had been in the bush close to a week. We were tired, smelly, frustrated at not being able to find the site, and under pressure to justify the support of the Chief Superintendent and ensure his reputation was not tarnished.

I posed a question, "What do you think people will say when we tell them what we had to go through to find the site?"

They pondered in silence.

"Imagine what it will be like for us when we locate it after all of this effort."

"How many people would give up right now? You know the answer ... most people would. Is that what we want to be; like most people, or do we want to show people what we're really made of?"

They looked at me, their eyes reflecting deep thought and the imagining of a far away place where they would be legends ... if only in their own minds.

The emotional shift that took place in that river bed as all three of us had the power to focus us on what it really meant to achieve the outcome we had so consistently given our full attention to under such challenging circumstances.

I have always lived by the philosophy that the difference between ordinary and extraordinary is that little extra. One of the biggest failures in life that many people experience is to give up when they are so close to the outcome.

I told them about a thought I'd had. "I think the results we get are directly proportional to the effort we put in. I believe we still have some more to give if we want to make this something really worthwhile."

Interestingly, one of the team put those words on a plaque they gave me when I transferred out of the unit. He remembered them.

With those words they joined me and we started the tracking from where it began.

That afternoon we located one of the largest drug operations ever seized, and the following day we led a force of about twenty officers and detectives in capturing every single person involved at the site without a single person getting hurt.

What kept us going was what we focused on when the going got really tough. While it was probably human nature to think about how physically hard it was or how we kept 'failing' to find the track, I know that it was the questions we asked that were the key to changing how we felt and cause us to finally push forward when we could easily have given up.

We questioned ourselves in a way that served us, we questioned our own thinking and were able to draw upon resources that at that point had been laying dormant.

# This Book

Look, I don't claim that this book has the answers for everyone suffering from PTSD. I just want to share what has worked for me and many people I've worked with.

To that end I've written the book with three outcomes in mind.

First, I want to sensitise you to the conversations you have in your head, more specifically the types of questions you ask yourself now. By doing that you will be in a better position to decide whether you should change how you communicate with yourself.

Second, I want to make you aware of how you can be the voice inside your head, and the types of questions you *can* ask that will have a tremendous effect they have on how you think, feel and behave. This gives you choices, options and other ways to communicate with yourself and the people around you. If you know what the choices are you can consciously make decisions about how you communicate. Master this aspect of thinking within yourself, and you have the foundations for better leadership of others.

And third, I want to pass on to you a list of well worn internal conversational questions you can use in a variety of situations; relationships, to teach, to change how you feel or change what you do, questions you can use at any time in common life situations. It's not my intention that you memorise these questions; rather I hope the book becomes a reference for you as you master the concept.

The ability to ask *great* questions, of both myself and others, has served to enhance *every* aspect of my life, personal and professional. The opportunity to share some of what I have learnt is very gratifying. I truly hope you find this an invaluable handbook for directing your mind with precision and proactively being the voice inside your head.

**George Lee Sye**
Australia, May 2025

> *'The greatest revolution of our generation is the discovery that human beings, by changing the inner attitudes of their minds, can change the outer aspects of their lives.'*
>
> **William James (1842 – 1910)**

# Controlling The Voice Inside

## Mind Experiments

Let me ask you this ... how do you know what time it is?

Think about that for a moment. Is it because you can see the hands on the clock and easily interpret what time it is by virtue of their position? My guess is that if you were going to give a technical answer it was going to be something like that.

How do you actually see what time it is?

With an understanding of physics, you would probably say that the reflection of light from the clock face to you allows you see the hands and numbers.

Now ponder this ..... if you could travel at the speed of light to the clock, what would you see then?

Because we see the reflection of light from the clock face, what you really see is the position of the hands as they were at the exact moment *when* the reflected light *left* the clock face.

We know light takes time to get to us, albeit quite quickly. If that is true, the actual position of the hands is slightly ahead of where they appear to be to you. If you travel to the clock at the speed of light you might see the hands of the clock move forward to their actual present position and the time would appear to move forward ever so slightly.

What if you could travel to the clock faster than the speed of light? Then what would you see? Well, if the previous answer were true, you would probably see the hands go backwards. You would get to the clock faster than the reflected light would get to you.

One final question ... would you be seeing the hands move backwards or would time actually reverse itself?

An interesting sequence of questions don't you think? These are the questions Albert Einstein asked himself during the thought experiments he conducted in coming up with his theory of relativity.

Regardless of what we might think of the answers, I find this thinking process fascinating. It's a great example of questions being used to empower a person to create something outstanding. Albert Einstein was a truly remarkable thinker and his primary tool was the ability to ask questions, not just of other people, but of himself.

> *'The important thing is not to stop questioning.'*
> **Albert Einstein (1879 - 1955)**

## What Do Questions Really Do?

Questions cause you to focus your mind; they direct your thinking and cause you to take notice of something specific. The brain does not know right from wrong, it knows only what it is focusing on. Let me talk you through an example of what I mean.

Take a moment to look around the room. Take a close look and notice everything you see that is red. When you've done that, come back to the page.

Now, what did you notice that was yellow? If you don't look around the room again, you may be able to recall a number of items, particularly if this is a room or area you frequent regularly, but in most cases you won't be able to recall them all.

When I asked you to take notice of everything red, that's exactly what you did. You filtered out everything that did not match the thing you were focused on. You did not take conscious notice of everything else that your eyes passed over in the room. In fact you experienced tunnel vision, not as a survival reaction to some event, rather it was in response to the question that was asked.

We communicate with ourselves continuously. Even if you're not aware of it, it is occurring at a subconscious level. We filter out all of the available information on the basis of how we communicate internally, and questions can form a significant part of that process.

In life, if your brain poses poor questions you get poor answers. If you're in the habit of asking questions of yourself like, 'Why can't I do this?' you filter out all of the reasons why you *can* do it. You get your mind to focus on one thing: all of the reasons why you cannot do it.

By contrast, if you ask 'What can I do?' or 'What could I achieve if I just have a go at this?', you redirect your thinking and focus your mind on finding answers to those questions.

When someone says 'We can't do that here,' or 'That doesn't work here,' those statements were created by looking for the reasons why it cannot be done or why it would not work.

The key is this; you must ask for what you want. You need to be aware of how you communicate to yourself, to be sensitive to what your questions cause you and others to focus on. To get a better answer, simply ask a better question.

My point here is that questions can and do control our mental focus. In dealing with the events of your life, past, present and even future, you need to ask questions that put you in a resourceful state, questions that serve you in some positive way rather than generate unnecessary negativity.

In situations where we want to help people learn, we can focus their minds on understanding or applying a new concept by asking quality questions. This is the basis of any form of good coaching.

In situations where we need to create or come up with some new idea, we can do that by having the right conversation within ourselves. As you already know, the foundation for that is the ability to ask good questions.

> *'The chains of habit are too weak to be felt until they are too strong to be broken.'*
>
> **Samuel Johnson (1709 - 1784)**
> **English Lexicographer, Critic and Writer**

# Learned Patterns of Thinking

Throughout our lives we are all constantly learning and unlearning patterns of behaviour. It's as if we record some MP3 file that we store in some filing system and then pull out to play in certain circumstances, or when we are exposed to some specific stimulus or trigger.

For example, when you get into an elevator do you have follow a particular pattern of behaviour? Do you run the 'How To Behave In An Elevator' script that guides you in a specific behaviour pattern?

Of course you do, everybody does. Regardless of the reason why, I would be willing to bet you follow a pattern of behaviour similar to this:

- You face towards the doors – you know the rules say it would be wrong to face the other occupants of the elevator.

- You dare not talk to anyone, even if you know the person.

- You can't move around, you have to be still.

- You stare up at the floor indicator lights or, if carrying something like a newspaper, you have to appear to be totally focused and absorbed in its content.

Does that sound like something you do?

## BE THE VOICE

Why we do this is not important at the moment. Let's focus on understanding how we form those scripts and make those files, how we learn those patterns of behaviour.

We learn them by repeating the behaviour until it becomes conditioned, even to the point where we perform the behaviour without even thinking about it. We just open the appropriate file and run the script when the circumstance is right, or a specific trigger is activated.

Driving a motor car is a great example of a learned or conditioned pattern of behaviour. How many times have you driven along a stretch of road and suddenly realised that you do not even remember driving for some period of time? You've driven a car so often that you can do it without thinking. You can do it unconsciously. Scary stuff!

Now the same is true of the way we communicate with ourselves and other people and, more specifically, how we ask questions and the types of questions we ask.

Most of the time we develop patterns that help keep us alive, patterns of behaviour that we know will move us away from harm or something we perceive to be painful, and take us towards something we perceive to be pleasurable. For example, in the elevator we are in such close proximity to people that complete strangers invade our personal space, so the pattern helps us to deal with that, helps us to move away from the feelings we get when a stranger is very close to you.

Sometimes we develop patterns of behaviour that are not so useful; patterns that hold us back, patterns that don't serve us in the way we intended.

For example, someone might express a pattern of finding fault with everything, identifying repeatedly what they don't like about things. At the most fundamental level they do this because being able to identify the danger or downside in something can keep them alive. It's a useful and very primal survival tool. The pattern has served them in the past so they keep using it and get very good at it.

Problems arise when this is the only characteristic they look for in any experience they have. They miss the other half of the situation; they only ever see the storm but never get to enjoy the sunshine. They stay alive but do not really get to enjoy the process.

It's simply a pattern of thinking they've learned to the point where it's unconscious. As I often remind people, most patterns of behaviour serve us, or have served us in some way in the past, but when we use the same pattern without thinking in every situation, that's when problems arise.

> *'You have one psychology, and you take that psychology to every situation you place yourself in. The first step in changing the outcomes you consistently get in life is to work on your psychology.'*

The following are some of the patterns of internal conversation that we must break if we are really going to take control over the quality of our lives.

## #1: A Pattern of Disempowerment

A disempowering question is one that ignores the value of an experience, puts you in an un-resourceful state or causes you to give up or not to try something that really would serve you. It robs you of the power you have inside.

Mental questions like these are disempowering.

- 'What do I hate about this?'

- 'Why can't I do this?'

- 'How is this worse than last time?'

- 'What would I rather be doing?'

Any internal communication that relieves you of responsibility for doing something and transfers blame or responsibility to someone else is also a disempowering question.

Questions like …..

- 'Why don't they do something about this?'

- 'When are they going to fix this?'

- 'Who is responsible for this?'

These questions shift responsibility to someone else. If everyone did that imagine what the state of your organisation or the state of the world would be.

The word 'power' means the ability to take action. When you have personal power, you do things. You're able to take action intended to achieve a specific outcome. Questions of this nature take away your power. They steal it and leave you in a disempowered state, a state in which you cannot move. You fail to take action when you really know you should.

You can't expect to achieve anything of significance in that state.

*'Nothing great was ever achieved without enthusiasm.'*
**Ralph Waldo Emerson (1803 - 1882)**
**American Essayist, Poet and Philosopher**

Let's go to the second pattern.

# #2: A Pattern of Victimisation

What do I mean by victimisation or victim? I mean people whose frame of reference is they have been wronged. Nothing is their fault, nothing good ever happens to them, they see themselves as victims. When you have these types of internal communications, you see yourself as a victim.

- 'Why does this always happen to me?'

- 'Why is my life so bad?'

- 'Why me?'

- 'Why can't I find the time?'

- 'Why am I so stressed?'

- 'Why can't I be as lucky as she is?'

I won't go on; I've no doubts you know the questions I'm talking about.

Questions of this nature take you to a place you do not want to be. They give you reasons for staying exactly where you are.

Ask and you shall receive. If you want to know why this always happens to you, all you need do is ask. Your brain will give you an answer, even if it's untrue.

It will tell you something like 'because you aren't smart enough', 'because you don't have some qualification', 'because you don't have the talent' or 'because people just don't like you'.

'Why can't I write a book?' ... because you don't have the time, because you don't know how to or because nobody will buy it. You'll get answers to these questions, and you know something, they will not be the answers you want or need. However, they will be the answers that bring you down emotionally and put you in a state where you don't get the results you really want.

Remember, what you ask for you will get.

BE THE VOICE

*'The greater part of our happiness or misery depends on our dispositions and not our circumstances.'*

**Martha Washington (1732 - 1802)**
**First Lady of the United States of America**

# #3: A Pattern of Stopping At The First Answer

When someone asks 'What can I do about this?', clearly they've asked a great question. If they then come up with one idea and analyse it to death and the idea does not work, what started as a good process has ended poorly.

How many times have you seen a group of people try to develop an idea for solving a problem and while ideas are being generated, someone starts the discussion in analysing a particular idea? In business there is wide recognition of the need to generate many ideas before any analysis starts.

Unfortunately, as individuals, we generally don't recognise the need to use that same approach.

If you want to tap into the real power of your brain, you have to explore as many answers as you can before you work out which answer is most appropriate. By pushing the thinking process beyond what appears to be obvious, you get to change the pattern of thinking that brought you to this point in time.

Always remember this:

*The pattern of thinking that got you to this point in your life, will not get you beyond it.*

The problems you experience now were created by your current thinking; real solutions come from a new level of thinking. By pushing yourself to find 10, 20 or even 30 different ways to deal with a problem, you are far more likely to find the answer to your question and more likely to find a way to move beyond your current situation.

## BE THE VOICE

*'When in doubt, make a fool of yourself. There is a microscopically thin line between being brilliantly creative and acting like the most gigantic idiot on earth. So what the hell, leap.'*

**Cynthia Heimel**
**American Feminist Writer (from Village Voice, 1989)**

### How are these patterns learned?

As I said, these patterns are learned through a process of conditioning. The mental pattern is repeated until it simply becomes the way you do it.

In many cases our exposure to the patterns of other people, particularly our parents, is what drives these patterns within ourselves. It can also cause us to become aware of certain patterns that produce negative outcomes, and as a result we make choices about doing the opposite.

Changing any pattern of thinking starts with you becoming aware of what you are doing. Conscious awareness puts you in a position where you have a choice about continuing with that pattern, or changing it.

# Questions Are The Key

Look, I definitely do not profess to have all the answers. But I know one thing; mental questions are the key to us consciously taking charge of that voice inside our heads.

To change what some experience means to you and how it affects you, you begin by asking new questions of yourself. This pattern can and will shift how you feel about things, and move you towards better outcomes.

People who achieve outstanding results communicate with themselves in a way that is different to those who don't get the same outcomes. They ask different questions of themselves. For example, an outstanding achiever trying to deal with some challenge in life would ask questions like - 'What can I do to solve this?' or 'What can I do to deal with this?' or 'How does this make me stronger?'

In everyday situations outstanding achievers are committed to the discipline of continual improvement so they ask questions like 'How can I make this even better?' or 'What can I do to improve?'

How did olympic swimming stars like Grant Hackett and Libby Lenton stay motivated to put in all of those crazy hours of doing laps in a pool, literally for years on end?

What process of thinking does a Rory McIlroy (Golf) or Aryna Sabalenka (Tennis) or Gordon Ryan (Brazilian Jiu Jitsu) use to get the discipline to practice and train day in, day out, year after year?

To make themselves take action consistently, outstanding achievers communicate with themselves in a way that causes them to move, they ask questions of a nature that others don't ask - questions like 'What must I do right now to get the outcomes I want?' or 'If I don't do this, what will that cost me?'

These questions lead to outstanding performance because they take people down the path of achievement, a path where they are empowered to take action and do it from a *resourceful* emotional state.

People who experience extraordinary intimate relationships ask outstanding questions; questions like 'How can I make this relationship even better?' or 'What do I appreciate about my lady?' or 'What can I do to make my man really feel loved?' Imagine what those questions do to someone's behaviour in a relationship. Those questions put them into a powerful state and get them to contribute to the relationship in a way that makes it extraordinary.

Outstanding coaches and trainers ask outstanding questions. If they want to create learning and challenge conventional thinking, they ask questions like 'What does this mean to you?' or 'How is this better than the way you've done it in the past?' They can generate understanding and teach the application of new concepts by asking questions. 'What did you do here that caused that outcome you didn't want?' and 'What would you change to get that different outcome that you do want?' 'How can you use this?' or 'How does this relate to what you do at work?'

Questions like these cause students to explore new concepts and understand how they can be applied to get different outcomes.

The greatest leaders of our time ask outstanding questions of their people. They ask questions that take people into the future like 'What's our vision for this company in three years?' and 'What do we need to do to make that a reality?' or 'What can you do to be a part of that?' That is the true role of a leader.

Influential leaders ask questions that change behaviour like 'How does this hold you back?' Other questions cause people to analyse what they are doing and why they should change. 'Why is making this vision a reality, an absolute must for us?' Questions like these drive people towards action.

Remember this famous quote about questions:

> *"Ask not what your country can do for you but what you can do for your country."*
> **President John F Kennedy**

The quality of your personal and working life can be taken to a completely new level through the use of questions. The right questions can enhance your performance as a parent, as a partner, as a son, as a daughter, as a friend, as a coach and as a leader of people.

Questions have the power to change what you think, feel and do. By taking control of the focus of your own mind and the mind of others you can become an even greater influence in the lives of people around you. You have the power to change how someone else feels, how they behave and the quality of their life.

## The Importance of Emotional State

Now some might say 'Wait a minute George, I don't talk to myself like that. New questions can't provide all of the answers I need in my life'.

Well …. is that not just a belief ?

A belief is nothing but a feeling of certainty about the truth of an idea or thought, but it does not mean the idea is actually true.

Would having that belief serve you in any way? How does believing you can't ask questions like that or talk to yourself in that way serve you? I don't think it does. That belief puts you in the wrong state to ask questions with any conviction, particularly those for which you think you do not have the answer.

Imagine if I asked 'How can I deal with this challenge?' or 'What can I do to make half a million dollars?' from a state of disbelief or uncertainty. Am I going to get the answers I need? ….. of course not. I have to be in a resourceful state to ask the question in the first place.

What if I ask those same questions with conviction and belief that answers will come, what would happen? I absolutely believe the answers do come, even if they don't come straight away.

I want to leave you with two thoughts:

> - You must communicate with yourself in an appropriate emotional state; you must do it with conviction, with belief – otherwise it's nothing but a façade; you won't get the answers.

> - Keep asking the question until the answers come. Just because they don't come straight away, does not mean they won't come. Keep asking. Never mistake a delay for a denial. The only time you are denied is if you stop asking.

## BE THE VOICE

*'The secret to making something work in your lives is first of all the deep desire to make it work; then the faith and belief that it can work; then to hold that clear definite vision in your consciousness and see it working out step by step, without one thought of doubt or disbelief.'*

**Eileen Caddy**
**Co-founder of 'The Findhorn Foundation', Scotland**

# Six Achievable Outcomes

As I said earlier, questions do one thing primarily – they direct or focus the attention of our minds. Questions asked well, move us away from where we do not want to be to a place where we can learn, extract value from an experience, and empower ourselves to take action.

A number of specific outcomes can be achieved through the use of good communication techniques based on questions. If you are aware of these outcomes you will more likely be able to identify useful questions you can use in a variety of circumstances. I want to share some of these with you.

*'Questions do one thing primarily ... they direct or focus the attention of one's mind.'*

## 1. Questions interrupt and re-direct thinking patterns.

The moment you ask a question, you change the focus of your mind. If you ask others a question you change their mental focus by interrupting the thinking pattern they were running and creating a new pattern.

Here's an example of what I mean.

Suppose a meeting facilitator was trying to generate solutions for solving a problem from a work team. What the facilitator would probably do is ask the team for ideas that they write on post-it notes and place on a flip-chart.

Eventually, the ideas start to dry up until the team gets to the point where they say they can think of no more.

You might've experienced this yourself. Meeting facilitators working on getting ideas from a team invariably find this happens. Ideas just stop flowing.

What would be the result if the facilitator asked a question like 'How would an astronaut solve this problem in space?' or 'What ideas could we get from how a team plays soccer?'

In the style of Edward De Bono, questions like these move people's minds laterally from a stuck point to a new starting point.

That lateral shift usually results in the generation of new and creative ideas. The old pattern of thinking would have been interrupted by the question with thoughts being taken to a new starting point.

Consider a person who is angry or upset about something.. What if you asked them a question completely unrelated to the situation like -'Before we go on, tell me does the flame of a lit match in zero gravity in space burn in a ball, or does the flame point in one direction like it does in gravity on earth?'

Such questions would [if not ignored] instantly interrupt their pattern of thinking, it would change their focus and could result in a change in their emotional state. When you change what people focus on you interrupt their thinking patterns and it can be used to change how they feel and even their behaviour.

When you ask a question of someone, they immediately start to search for the answer. The quality of the question you ask will determine the quality of the answers you get. Remember what I said earlier, a question guides or directs the mind down a particular path. All we need to do is choose the path that best serves us.

What else do questions do?

## 2. Questions determine how people filter and sort through all of the information that's available to them.

What does it feel like to wear a watch on your wrist? How much pressure does your left shoe apply to your foot? What sound can you hear right now? What do you love about your job? What is the most enjoyable thing you have done in the past 5 years?

By the time I asked you the last question, no doubt you forgot about what it felt like to have a watch on your wrist.

So much information is available to us at any single moment, it would be impossible to take notice of it all. We are limited by what's known as channel capacity. That concept is often referred to as "Miller's Law," a name that stems from a famous 1956 paper by psychologist George A. Miller titled - The Magical Number Seven, Plus or Minus Two: Some Limits on Our Capacity for Processing Information.

Miller proposed that the capacity of our short-term memory (or working memory) is limited to about 7 items (plus or minus 2) — meaning that most people can hold between 5 and 9 discrete pieces of information in their minds at once. This applies to myriad types of information that we perceive and take in through the senses.

More recent research has suggested the actual number may be closer to 4 for certain tasks. Experiments I've done in large conferences indicate to me that it is closer to 4 or 5.

Regardless of the number, Miller's framework remains a foundational concept in understanding the limitations of human information processing.

I mention this here because Miller's concept of limited cognitive capacity can help explain why people who've experienced trauma or emotionally intense events often focus almost exclusively on the negative aspects, even when positive elements were also present.

Let me explain it this way.

## We Have A Naturally Limited Attention Span

As Miller proposed, people can only give attention to a small number of pieces of information at any one time. In highly emotional or threatening situations, the brain prioritises survival-relevant details such as danger, fear, embarrassment, betrayal, loss and the like. These are perceived as critical for future self-protection.

## We Have A Negativity Bias

Our brains are naturally wired to give more weight to negative information than positive information. This bias means that among all of the information and details available, we focus on a limited number of things and negative elements often dominate.

## We Unconsciously Engage In Emotional Tagging

When a traumatic event occurs, the amygdala (which is emotion center of the brain) tags certain details as emotionally significant so those details area easier to recall later. This is often at the expense of other, more neutral or positive aspects of an experience.

## Cognitive Overload and Filtering

In traumatic moments, people may filter out less emotionally intense information simply to cope. Because the brain can't process everything at once, it stores and recalls the loudest, most emotionally charged parts, and this usually ends up being the negative ones.

Let's apply this to our own experiences. We select certain pieces of available information and ignore everything we consider to be unimportant at that time.

Just think for a moment about the travesty that has occurred in the world. There have been an incredible number of deaths in the fighting in Ukraine and in the Gaza, not only military personnel but innocent and unarmed civilians. Hundreds of thousands of people lost their lives during the Tsunami that hit Indonesia and parts of India on New Years day 2005. Countries like Australia and the United States have experienced an unacceptable number of deaths in motor vehicle accidents and, on top of all of this, we are seeing a continuous increase in the number of deaths in western societies from cancer. Cast your mind back a few years, we saw the tremendous suffering in New Orleans in the aftermath of Hurricane Katrina.

As you think about this, how does that make you feel? I'd suggest that it could get quite depressing. Having filtered all of the events we could focus on, I've obviously chosen only those that fit within the death and destruction category.

Now, think about all of the great things that have occurred over the past 18 months. How many babies were born? What a wonderful part of human existence that is. How many extraordinary acts of courage were you witness to or did you read about? How many people regained their sight in the past five years because of the Fred Hollows Foundation? What positive event occurred in your life that you will always remember, something you will cherish for many years to come? What was your most memorable moment with a person you love?

As you think about these things, notice how you feel? All you are doing is ignoring all of the things that make you feel bad and taking notice of the things that make you feel good.

Human beings are filtering and deletion machines, we do it continuously, ultimately for the purpose of survival. Our brain is constantly trying to determine what things mean so it can move us away from danger and keep us alive. It looks for and takes notice of anything that might harm us or cause us pain. When it finds it we then change our behaviour in such a way as to move away from it. It also takes notice of anything we value or anything that brings us pleasure in some way. Anything else is ignored, its just noise.

We have to do this to get through each day safely without being totally overwhelmed. The problem is that many people tend to look for the pain or downside of an experience first, which is okay by the way, but when they find something they stay focused on that adverse perspective. They never get to the up side, which does exist. You must agree, there are pros and cons for everything.

When this happens the person's focus is disproportionately drawn to the negative side of life's experience and they spend a disproportionate amount of time in a negative emotional state as a result.

When you feel sad or unhappy you are ignoring all of the reasons you have to feel good, and are taking notice of the reasons why you should feel sad. By contrast, if you feel good you are ignoring all of the reasons why you should feel bad.

If you don't want to do something, you're ignoring all of the reasons for doing it. However, if you do want to do something you are ignoring all of the reasons for not doing it and taking notice of the reasons why you should. I hope that makes sense to you.

This happens in our home life and at work. If you experience resistance at work for some change in which you are involved, the people resisting you are only taking notice of all the reasons why they should resist the change. You are focused on why the change must happen and probably cannot understand why 'They just don't get it'; it is so obvious to you.

It is all about perspective, and perspective is often based on what we consciously and unconsciously notice. To get other people to change, you first must change what they notice and give attention to.

If you want to change what you or someone else notices, you ask questions that take their attention to those things.

*'The mind is its own place, and in itself can make a heaven of hell, and a hell of heaven.'*

**John Milton (1606 – 1674)**
**English Poet**

## 3. Questions can change the meaning you give to any experience.

Mastering meaning; this is one of the most important skills you will ever develop in dealing with the more negative experiences of your life.

Two people can have exactly the same experience, yet respond in entirely different ways and experience entirely different emotions. One person says the experience is an exciting adventure while another person totally disagrees; they call the experience a terrifying ordeal. There are two perspectives to everything, a positive view and a negative view.

The perspective we choose to take for any experience determines how we feel about that experience.

I told you about my experience finding my dad after he committed suicide. I worked hard to come to terms with that situation and one of the ways I did it was by changing what the experience meant to me. You might ask 'How on earth do you change what this means, it's the death of your father?'

When I finally came to terms with what he did, I asked myself some very important questions. 'What can I learn from this?', 'How can I use this experience in a positive way in my own life?' and 'How does this experience make me a stronger and better person?'

One question that really worked for me, I still use the form of this question today when I work with other people is this; 'If he, my father in this case, was looking down at me right now and able to give me one piece of advice, what would he say to me?'

My father was a very strict man so I knew he would probably tell me to stop blubbering and get back to work; something of that tone.

By asking these questions and taking control of what I focused on, I got answers that changed my state. It helped turn what was a personal disaster into a learning experience. I believe it also shaped me and gave me knowledge that I can use to positively impact other people's lives.

I mean, I'm using the experience right now. I can tell you there is no experience in my life that I can't make meaningful in some way; all I do is consciously ask myself the questions that enable me to take a perspective that serves me. You can do the same, if you choose to.

> *'Your experiences are what you choose them to be. Your habits, your character, your responses are entirely your choice.'*

What you focus on determines what something means. If you concentrate on all of the negative aspects of an experience, how it hurts you, how it's painful, and what it will cost you; you give it a negative meaning and, as a result, you feel lousy.

If you give attention to all the lessons you can take away and the ways that experience can ultimately serve you, or on how this will shape you as a person and make you even stronger; you attach some positive meaning to the experience. As a result, you feel positive emotions.

The goal is to put yourself in a resourceful state and you can do that by taking control of that voice inside your head and asking yourself the right questions.

Remember this, the only meaning any experience has is the one you choose to give it. If you want to change what an experience means, ask a new question.

> *'Some men see things as they are and say, 'Why?' I dream things that never were and say, 'Why not?'*
>
> **George Bernard Shaw (1856 – 1950)**
> **Irish Dramatist, Essayist and Critic**

## 4. Questions can get people to draw upon and use the power they possess within.

If you ask, 'Why can't I do that?' you tap into the resources that stop you moving forward and taking action. By contrast, if you ask 'How can I do this?' you draw upon resources to help you take action and actually do it.

By focusing your mind in a direction with good questions, you get good answers. You unleash the resources that you have within already.

What do you think it is that makes the difference between those who do achieve amazing results and those who do not?

The research I've undertaken over the past decades in answering this question has proven to me beyond a shadow of a doubt that outstanding achievers communicate with themselves in a way that is very different from others. This is the difference that makes the difference.

Achievers might have some talent that not everybody has or they might have potential in a specific area. But guess what, there are many people out there with the same talent and potential who don't have the same level of success. No doubts you know people like that.

The difference is that high achievers communicate with themselves in such a way they exploit their talent. They take action to the extent that they really tap into their true potential. Most people just do not do that. Most fail to question themselves as high achievers do.

Truth is, you already have the power within, an incredible reserve of resources; you can tap into that reservoir by having a very different conversation with yourself, by asking new questions.

In 2004 I wrote my first real book. It was a 670 page body of knowledge about the technical elements of a specific business improvement initiative called 'Six Sigma'. During that period I spent an enormous amount of time traveling and presenting training courses in various parts of the world. I clocked up more than 1 million frequent flyer points in a single year. At one point I ran a block of twenty-eight week-long training courses, all consecutively. That was one hectic period of time.

Now, I am not an academic, I have no special skill. I am just an ordinary guy. In fact, I started my working life at 15 as a builder's labourer for a couple of years. I then spent the next eight years getting my motor mechanic's ticket and working as a tradesman.

Most people with a schedule like I had at the time would say there is no time to do what I did with the book. So how did I get to write it?

The answer lies in the way I communicated with myself. What I did was ask one question of myself every single morning for almost one and a half years, that question was this: 'What will I do today to move closer to completing this book?' Every single day I arrived at the same answer – 'Start writing and complete at least one paragraph'. In 2004, a book popped out and people said 'You're so lucky you had time to do that'.

It definitely was not luck. It was simply the discipline to get into momentum by starting to write when I didn't feel like writing.

I repeated the process for the second edition of that book, and recorded 1,296 hours of typing to produce what is now an 830 page monster text book. I simply kept my mind focused on the objective and just did the work.

Remember, the resources already reside within; that voice inside your head can help you tap into those, or not, depending on whether you control it.

BE THE VOICE

*At the Cafe / Bar Where The 2nd Book Edition Was finished*

A point always to remember is this, momentum plays a big part in how this works. When you take control of your internal voice and ask yourself empowering questions, you get on a roll. You get good answers, you put yourself in a resourceful state, you take action, you get results, your internal conversation is more empowering and slowly but surely it becomes habitual. As you get greater results in your life the process of getting them becomes a learned behaviour.

The opposite is also true. If you let that internal voice look for the easy way out by asking lousy questions, you get lousy answers, you remain in an un-resourceful state and fail to tap into the power you really do possess inside. You get yourself on a cycle of poor questions, poor answers, feel bad, take lousy action and get lousy results. The outcome reinforces any self doubt and the downward spiral is then in full motion.

This is not where you want to be, nor is it where you have to be.

If you want to take control, you must be sensitive to how you communicate with yourself, particularly the types of questions that run around your mind.

So what other outcomes can you get with questions?

## 5. Questions can cause you to change your own perception.

> *'Discovery consists of seeing what everybody has seen and thinking what nobody has thought.'*
>
> **Albert Szent-Györgyi (1893 - unknown)**
> **Hungarian-born American Biochemist**

The role of a coach is fundamentally to influence a person's thinking. By changing what and how a person thinks about something, new behaviours can result. The question is how do they do that?

Obviously one way to influence a person's thinking is to tell them what they should know or tell them how they should think or behave. This approach only works if the coach is knowledgable, and the student is prepared to actually change because they've been told something.

My experience with people is that the best way to influence someone's thinking isn't to tell them, but rather to get them to find the answers themselves through asking the right questions.

For example, let's say I was coaching you and had suggested some action, and in response you said to me 'I can't do that'. How could I influence your thinking?

## BE THE VOICE

If I took the tell approach I would say 'Yes you can,' or 'Lots of people have said that but discovered they were wrong'. The problem with this approach is that I am telling you what I believe. That is my reality, not yours. So you would be unlikely to behave consistently with those beliefs.

On the other hand, I could ask you a range of questions with the intention of you finding your own answers. What if I were to ask questions like these:

'What can you do now that you once thought you couldn't do?'

'Think about your past for a minute, when have you said those same words but ended up being mistaken and you really could do it?'

These types of questions prompt you to come up with the answers yourself. You begin to take notice of things that you were ignoring.

The fact is I don't have to convince you of the truth of any of those answers, they are your reality. As a result you're more likely to behave consistently with what you say and believe.

We can also coach ourselves to think in new ways. Albert Einstein did exactly that through his 'thought experiments'.

At any moment I could challenge my own thinking by asking 'possibility' questions like these:

- 'Is it possible there's another way of approaching this?'

- 'Is it possible that this perspective is limited or could lead me down the wrong path?'

- 'Is it possible that I am wrong?'

By taking control of the voice inside my head and asking questions like this, I open my heart and mind to the possibility there is another way.

## BE THE VOICE

Much of what we do every day requires a logical process of thinking to come up with an answer or make some decision. What we must be conscious of is the fact that any thinking process, logical or not, starts from a point of perception.

Here's an example. Let's say I need to solve the problem of my car overheating. I think the cause is a radiator issue, so the logic I apply in solving this problem will lead to solutions such as 'buy a new radiator' or 'flush out the radiator' or maybe 'install a new or larger capacity radiator'.

What if the real cause was actually a corroded water pump impeller, then my solutions would not solve the problem.

There's probably nothing wrong with the logic I applied in identifying solutions, but my perception at the start was flawed, therefore I ended up with the wrong answers.

The point I am making is simply this; the logic may well be correct, but if your perception at the beginning of the process is incorrect, you will end up with the wrong answer or make the wrong decision in any case.

Another simple example of this can be found in a mathematics examination question. Suppose the student starts the mathematical calculation process by incorrectly writing down one of the numbers, say they write down the number to the 4th decimal point, the correct logic will result in the wrong answer if the examiner used 6 decimal points to determine the correct answer. This happened to my son during an online university examination. His mathematics was perfect, yet he was marked wrong because he begin a logical mathematical process with an incorrectly written number.

By challenging your own perception with possibility types of questions you become your own coach.

There is one last outcome that I want to discuss.

## 6. Questions can cause us to make connections between two seemingly unrelated concepts.

We can greatly accelerate our ability to learn and apply concepts by making these connections. For example, if I look at a game of football and ask 'How is that like business and how can I learn from it?' I get my brain to start searching for the elements of the game that relate in some way to business. I might get answers like this.

- Footballers work as a team.

- They have a common direction and their actions are aligned towards a common outcome.

- When they make many mistakes in the fundamentals, they tend to lose the game. In order to win they have to get the little things right as a foundation to the big plays.

- When the rules are being challenged they use a referee.

- Every player has a specific identity and role to play.

I could explore this much further and come up with many ways to connect the two. In fact, it's not hard to make a connection between any two things irrespective of how unrelated they might seem to be. When I ask 'How is this like this?', I start to create that connection.

Here's an example of how I've used this in coaching people. I often ask a group of people in leadership programs to pick up a permanent marker and draw a circle on their forehead. Yep, you guessed it, people resist, they won't do it. That opens the group up to some interesting learning points.

>    Q. 'So tell me why you won't do it?'
>
>    A. 'I don't want to write on myself.'
>
>    Q. 'What would it take to get you to do it?'

A. 'Well, I want to know why I should and where this is heading.'

Q. 'How is this like a situation where you tell people to change their behaviour in the workplace?'

A. 'I guess they need to know why the change is important and what the outcome is before they're likely to do it.'

Q. 'What if I asked you to stick a post-it note on your forehead, would you be prepared to do that instead of writing on yourself?'

A. 'Yes.'

Q. 'What's different about sticking the post-it note on your forehead and writing on your forehead with the marker?'

A. 'I can take the post-it note off easily.'

Q. 'How is this like how people respond to change in your workplace?'

A. 'People are more likely to do things that they can easily undo.'

The conversation can go on but the point is this, by making connections between two concepts we can accelerate learning in a way that people genuinely understand a new concept. The most effective way to do that is through questioning.

Let's recap what we've covered.

There are **Six Outcomes** that can be achieved through the use of questioning.

    1. Questions interrupt thinking patterns.

    2. Questions determine how people filter the information in their environment, what they take notice of and what they ignore.

3. Questions can change the meaning you give to any experience.

4. Questions get you to draw upon internal resources.

5. Questions can cause a change in perception; and finally

6. Questions can help create links between any two situations for learning purposes.

# Four Types of Questions

There are any number of ways to describe the different types of questions we might ask of ourselves and others, to positively enhance either their lives or our own lives.

In order to keep this as simple as possible I've categorised those questions into four different types.

This first type is the one I believe is the most important if we want to experience a quality life. It deals with emotions.

# 1. Changing How We Feel About Experiences
## Reframing Past Experiences

I was doing uniformed patrol early one morning with my partner Dave. This was back in the late 1980s. It was around 1 am towards the end of our 6pm to 2am shift when we were travelling along Bunda Street in Cairns. I was driving, Dave was in the passenger seat. Things had started to quieten down and we'd got accustomed to just cruising along the back streets looking for strange and suspicious activities, and chatting away as we normally did.

As we neared the intersection with the main road that takes cars south out of town, a man ran out into the street in front of us waving his arms and yelling.

"Someone's been shooting in the house!" He shouted as he pointed back to his right at an old two storey dwelling.

I stopped the patrol car right beside the man so he was at the open window of the passenger side. Dave tried to settle the guy down and understand what the problem was. "Slow down, tell me exactly what has happened?"

"Someone was firing a gun in that house." And again he pointed to the old two storey house. He was agitated, yet he seemed to me to be sober and genuinely concerned.

Dave continued the conversation to get as much information as possible. But both Dave and I were quite wary about the situation, it seemed to me it was possible this was some kind of a set up. Dave had the same thoughts. The fact we were in a low income area of town, and it was dark and quiet with little lighting, only reinforced this wariness.

Dave directed the guy to stay at the intersection behind us, and I reversed the car and parked it on the side of the road just beyond the intersection.

We got out of the car, drew our pistols, and slowly made our way towards the building, all the while watching for signs of an ambush. I noticed some light was coming from inside the top floor but there was no movement that I could see.

The building was an old timber structure set on wooden poles, a pretty typical design for older houses in the northern part of Australia. The ground floor was more of a garage and open storage area with timber slat walls and a bare concrete floor. The stairway to the top floor was internal, and to get to it we had to move underneath the house.

As we approached the stairway, my heart was beating fast and my thoughts were still pondering the idea that this was an ambush. It was eerily silent except for the sound of my own pulse.

We cleared the ground floor and then moved without speaking towards the stairway. The first thing I noticed was the blood. The red fluid was running down the stairs and dripping through the gaps onto the concrete below. It was dripping through small gaps in floorboards beyond the top of the stairs as well. My pulse quickened, every hair follicle on my skin was standing up.

Dave and I slowly made our way towards the bottom step area. Covering our arcs, I carefully made my way up the stairs, avoiding the pooling blood as best I could. Dave followed.

At the top of the stair was a female, she was lying motionless in a pool of what seemed to be her own blood, much of which was running onto and down the stairs.

There were no weapons near her so I continued to move into the house. As we moved through we found two more people also motionless on the floor in pools of blood. Both had what appeared to be gunshot wounds to the head and upper body.

As we cleared further, we came upon a fourth person deeper in the house. The man had a rifle near him, he moved slightly and moaned as he lay on his side, covered in his own blood. He also had a gunshot wound to the head.

We had no choice but to finish clearing the house before we attended to anyone. It was only then that we did a quick check where we confirmed that the first three people, two women and a man, did not have pulses. The fourth man had been moaning and moving when I first came across him, but now he was still. I desperately tried to find a pulse but couldn't. Blood was everywhere. I remember describing it as a 'paint party' where buckets of red paint had been splashed all over the place.

I had the thought that I had to try something, and the only person whom I believed I had a chance with was the fourth guy that I'd heard moaning, but now had no pulse. So I rolled him onto his back and started chest compressions. It was horrible, as I pumped his chest more blood came out of wounds in his head. Part of the lower part of his face was missing and there was no way I could do any form of resuscitation without some sort of equipment. So I stopped.

When the ambos turned up, they confirmed there was nothing we could have done.

The feeling of helplessness was overwhelming. I remember looking around, seeing the two women and two men, and thinking what a waste this was. I was confident at the time, and it turned out to be true, that it was a murder suicide where the fourth person we found was the shooter. But the blood, man oh man, we were covered in it.

Back then, there was no debrief for this. We simply did the job, completed the required paperwork and went back to work.

The way Dave and I dealt with it was to talk about it. We agreed it was a good thing that it was us two who were first on the scene for this job, rather than a first year officer. Distorted or not, we believed we were better equiped to deal with it, both tactically and emotionally.

I always approached jobs of this nature from a "what's done is done" mindset. I can't change the past, I can only control what happens now and in future. And given this is what I would categorise as an 'exposure' type of event, one where there is no real personal loss that I can perceive, only exposure to circumstances; it can be turned into a learning experience by asking the right questions - what did we do well, what did we learn, what would we do differently next time?

The positives for me were that we had each other's back, we did the best we could to avoid an ambush, we sequenced our actions correctly, we did our absolute best to try and help the victims where we could, and we learnt we needed more equipment to deal with the CPR aspects of an event like this.

I know I've mentioned this previously, but let me make this point again. A question like 'How does this serve me?' puts me in a state where I look for ways to use the experience. 'How can I learn from this?' or 'What can I learn from this?' turns it into a learning experience. It effectively flips your frame of reference from a terrible experience to a learning experience.

'How will this make me stronger?' causes me to recognise that this experience is one that will shape me in some way as a person and gives the experience a new meaning.

When you have these types of conversations with yourself, you can positively alter what you associate with most experiences. If you can link value to an experience, you will be in a far better position both from a thinking and an emotional perspective.

I said "most experiences" because there are some that are not quite so easy to reframe.

## Reframing Loss (Perceived and Real)

Dave and I were exposed to circumstances. However, some experiences are more than exposure. When they result in perceived or real loss, I've found they are more difficult to deal with.

My buddy, let's call him by his call sign - Case, has been a police officer for over thirty years. Case was exposed to a traumatic event where it was more than just exposure. You need to hear the story in his words.

*It was 1997. I was working nightshift with Phil, a very switched on and professional Sergeant who had recently taken promotion back to uniform, after having spent several years as an investigator at the Homicide Squad.*

*First job for the night was to back up the van crews at a serious assault in a set of high-rise flats. I think the job was on or close to the 20th floor.*

*We arrived with the other crews and went straight to the flat where we were let inside by a bloke in his 50's. There were several people in the flat who pointed us to a bedroom which had the door closed. Phil and I went in with the other police who were there. On the bed was a male in his 20's, laying on his back staring at the ceiling. Near him on the floor was a young woman who had clearly been stabbed multiple times in her chest, shoulders, neck, face and arms. She was bleeding heavily and laying in a pool of her own blood.*

*There were others in the flat with us but I can't really remember who was doing what at this stage. There were a couple of other Police members in the room with us and somebody put cuffs on the 20 year old male.*

*I can't remember much of the lead-up to this, but we had been told by one of the family members that he had been fighting with her in the room and was responsible for her injuries.*

*All of this stuff usually happens pretty fast. The young woman, Sandra, was conscious but clearly struggling to move and breathe at this stage. I remember she turned her head and looked at me with a pleading and terrified look on her face. She was a beautiful young Columbian woman. She had tears in her eyes and was trying to speak.*

*It was obviously still an active crime-scene and the ambo's had arrived at this stage but weren't able to come to the flat until they were cleared by us. Phil looked at me and said "get her to the ambos mate, we don't have time to wait." I scooped her up, I put both arms under her like when you pick up a sleeping kid ,and I started running for the lift well.*

*When I dream about this story, which I still do occasionally, the facts change a little bit in the dream. Over time I guess things get a bit distorted. Sometimes I think I carried her like this the whole way down in the lift but I think I actually met the ambo's in the foyer when the lift doors opened. They had a stretcher and I put her on it. I remember that clearly, just not where it happened.*

*Sandra never stopped looking at me the whole time, she had tears flowing out of her eyes and blood dripping and running from everywhere. She said "help me" a few times, but she more mouthed the words, because the words weren't really coming out.*

## BE THE VOICE

*Despite this both she and I knew she was going to die. She was so frightened. She had so many stab wounds to her upper body that her chest must've been filling up with blood and air and she had blood bubbling out of her mouth by this stage. She was having more and more difficulty breathing and trying to speak. Eventually she stopped breathing. She was still looking straight at me when that happened. She never stopped looking at me. She was begging me to save her. I was trying to re-assure her that she would be ok in the calmest and most gentle voice I could.*

*The Ambo's were now working furiously on her but we all looked at each other and they confirmed what I knew without saying a word. They are such pro's though. They never give up. I don't know how anyone can do what they do and not be destroyed by it. I love the Ambo's.*

*They kept working but I remember them saying to me that the only hope was to get her into surgery as soon as possible. In truth, we all knew it was hopeless. Sandra never closed her eyes, but she was gone. I remember helping the ambo's get her into the back of their ambulance and they took off with lights and sirens to the hospital which was only about a kilometre up the road. I remember thinking maybe they can work some miracle there.*

*By the time I went back into the foyer of the flats a couple of the other members had brought the 20 year old male down to the foyer and he was pretending to be catatonic, laying on the floor staring blankly. He obviously thought he could check out and we would believe he had no memory of the incident.*

*He was pretty much uninjured from what I can remember although his hands were covered in blood. Phil asked me to travel in the ambulance with him and not let him out of my sight. We loaded the piece of shit into the back of the ambulance. He was a complete dead-weight. I wanted to bash him to death then and there. I was ropable, furious. But I didn't, I switched back into pro-mode and helped the ambo's get him loaded and take him for assessment.*

## BE THE VOICE

*I sat in the back of the ambulance with him and helped the lads wheel him into a cubicle at the hospital emergency department.*

*I sat with him for the next few hours and took notes of literally everything. He peeked out of the corner of his eye a few times to see who was there and when he saw me there he just went right back to pretending he was catatonic. Upstairs, a whole bunch of specialists were no doubt working their arses off trying to repair the girl he destroyed.*

*A few Doctors came in and examined him and confirmed there was nothing wrong with him. After one of the consults he started talking to me, saying "what have I done?" Telling me that she was going to leave him, that he had brought her out from Columbia and paid for all her holidays and let her move in and they were going to get married.*

*It was a massive "woe is me" fucking sob-story. It was like he thought I was going to understand his point of view, which was clearly that he owned her. She was his property, he had invested money in her and she had no right to leave him.*

*He was a fourth year law student. Phil (that guy is a legend) pointed the homicide squad guys to some of his law books that were in his room where he murdered her. He had post-it-notes and other notes stuck in the law books where he had recently been studying Automatism. This was what he was trying to run with, his defence for murder.*

*He actually thought he could outsmart everyone with his knowledge of the law to beat a murder charge. It turns out it was pretty good evidence of pre-meditation. That and my evidence of his behaviour at the hospital was pretty important in convicting him.*

*I'll never forget getting up into the box at the Supreme Court and giving my evidence. It was the old-school Supreme Court. You literally climbed up into a fancy box and stood up at eye level with the Judge and Jury, on full display. It was so hard to choke back the emotion during my evidence, but I managed. He got 27 years, she died. I think she was 19 or 20.*

## BE THE VOICE

*I had pretty much filed this memory away into the "too hard basket" in my head. Right down the bottom, at the back, where nobody is allowed to go. You come right back into work the next night and go again. We never sat around and talked about stuff back then. We would usually just go and have a drink together then go home. Go home to our partners and families and try to act normal, like you had a normal shift. But some shifts were far from normal.*

Let me add something in here. How is one supposed to deal with that? Do the job and then just go on like nothing happened. Back in those days everything was about the job. Not just in policing, but all first responder and defence force roles. There was pretty much zero consideration built in the system to care for the well being of the people doing those jobs.

Talking to Case about this event, it was interesting for us to realise we both had the perception that if we talked about these things in an emotional way we would be considered a 'pussy'. I even had that thought about others, so deeply ingrained was that perception back then.

Case's story continues.

*Years later, one afternoon, I was buying firewood for the home. I had filled my trailer up and was waiting in the foyer to pay for my wood and there was another bloke standing in the foyer waiting to do the same. We both recognised each other. I asked him if he was in the job and he said yeah, I am. We introduced ourselves, his name was Mick, a great bloke.*

*He said "the last time I remember seeing you, you had blood all over you at those flats. Do you remember that?"*

*I remembered, it all came flooding back in that instant, but I didn't let on that I was affected by it. I just said "oh yeah, that girl that was murdered".*

*We didn't really talk about it any more, we just had a bit of friendly banter and went home. It was a conversation killer. I got home that night and unloaded my firewood. It was all really hitting me hard by then and I remember just hoping that nobody would come out of the house to help me unload the wood because I couldn't talk. I was trying not to cry. I wondered if Mick was affected by it like I was. I completely lost it that night and bawled to myself in the shower. Absolutely bawled.*

*This memory can still and often does come up and fill me with emotion. I still have vivid dreams about her face from time to time. Sometimes several times in a week and sometimes not for months. I wish I could've done more to help her. I relive this memory and imagine getting the call a bit sooner, arriving a bit sooner and preventing it.*

*I'll never forget this girls face. I'll never forget her eyes looking at mine. It is a horrible memory. Sandra.*

Those memories never leave a person. The more emotional the event is, the stronger it is wired into your head. The question is, how does one deal with that and reframe it in some positive way so at least when the memory comes up, it doesn't drag you down into a state of depression?

Remember Miller's Law?

The first step is to recognise that the mental filtering process we go through is normal. The human brain has a limited capacity to process experiences, and when exposed to significant emotional stress, it prioritises loss / threat-related details.

Yes, our brains do what they are wired to do: they focus our attention on the parts of the experience that feel dangerous or painful so we can protect ourselves. But that also means other parts of the experience have probably been filtered out.

The second step is to fill in some memory gaps, maybe a better term is 'acknowledgement gaps'.

We need to consider or acknowledge some neutral or even positive memories that might have been overwritten or ignored.

## BE THE VOICE

By zooming out a little and viewing the experience from a further distance away, is it possible there were moments, even small moments or details that you wouldn't consider to be negative?

The answer is always yes.

Case did everything he possibly could to help Sandra. He did not desert her and she clearly knew and appreciated that. The incredibly skilled ambo's did everything they could, they threw everything they had into trying to save her. Phil had Case's back. The shit bag who did it was caught and convicted, he didn't get away with it. Experienced people attended the scene rather than inexperienced trainees who might have not have been able to function after it. Case has been able to function effectively in spite of this, demonstrating incredible resilience. That makes him even more exceptional in coaching and guiding others through experiences of this type.

It's the acknowledgement of those details that at least gives the memory of an event like this more balance.

The third step is to remember, and if you need to talk about the event, to integrate both the pain and the value of the experience into the story. This doesn't mean denying the bad, it simply means reducing the exclusive hold of the painful elements on one's attention.

*"Yep, that was a tough time, but not every part of it was wasted or negative. I came away with scars, but also with strength and insight. My resilience is much stronger because of it."*

The conversational questions that can help in circumstances like this one are in this form:

- 'Is it possible I am only seeing all of the painful details of this experience to the exclusion of everything else?'

- 'If I move back from the event a little, what other details can I consider that are either neutral or even positive in this event?'

- 'When I talk about this event, what can I say that would balance the pain of it with the value it presented?'

This was how, in later years, I dealt with my childhood experiences with those predatory arseholes who took some of my innocence as a kid. I balanced the bad memories with acknowledgement of what I took away as positives and how it helped me recognise those types of people and become a better protector of my kids.

## Contrasting

Another way to change how you feel about any situation is to tap into the power of contrasting. To contrast you simply ask questions like 'How could this be worse?' or 'Who's in a worse situation than I am?', or anything that gets you to view your situation from the frame that it could be worse than it is.

What other situations or experiences might challenge us? How about in relationships?

## Relationships

Questions can have a profound effect on the quality of your most intimate relationship. So how can questions do that?

Let's recognise that generally speaking, many issues in relationships stem from the other person doing or saying something we don't like. We get upset or feel offended and even end up arguing.

These are what I've found to be the most useful questions one can bring to a relationship if you want to change how you feel about those awkward moments.

- 'What else could this actually mean?'

- 'What other meaning could I give this?'

## BE THE VOICE

By asking questions like these, you open your mind to the possibility that some behaviour you dislike, might not mean what you think it means.

Here's an example. Suppose my wife doesn't come home at the time I expect her. A couple of hours go by and she doesn't ring me. I begin to have negative thoughts about why she's not yet home. 'She's not here because she doesn't respect me', 'She doesn't think I'm important enough to come home on time', 'She hasn't called because she doesn't really care', 'She's more interested in something or someone else'.

How do you suppose that thinking would affect my emotional state? How would that thinking affect how I behave when my wife does get home? She'll arrive home and I'll be all worked up, I rip it into her about how this has hurt me and how I've been put out.

Would that hurt the relationship? Of course it would, here I am ripping into her, my frame of mind being this - If I'm upset then she better be upset too.

Here's what's interesting, something about human behaviour you need to keep in mind.

If I do that, I'm causing her pain for doing exactly what I wanted her to do – come home. Think about it, she comes home and an emotionally charged argument begins. She associates pain with coming home, pain to the process of trying to relate to me, pain to the relationship. Do that multiple times and you have serious problems.

We've all done that, haven't we?

When we do this, we are reacting to the situation in one of two ways.

First, we might be reacting to our past. We've experienced this in the past in some way, where this situation occurred because one partner didn't care or they were having an affair. It might have even been a movie. We associate this with that, and then react accordingly.

## BE THE VOICE

It's certainly not fair to do that. Both you and your partner deserve more. The presumption of innocence is ignored when we think it is really about us. The truth is in most cases your partner is probably beating him or herself up over not being here on time so you need not get in on the act as well. It's actually not about you. It's really about your partner trying to meet his or her own needs.

The second reason we do this is we are reacting to what it would mean if we did it.

The truth is, we respond to the perception we have of a situation rather than the reality; we respond to the meaning we give it. I have zero idea what goes on in her mind before she gets home so I have no idea of the truth.

The key to success in a relationship is to learn to manage meaning.

By asking, 'What else could this mean?' or 'What other meaning could I give this situation?', and then looking for other meaning, you move yourself away from what is really hallucination and open your mind to positive meanings.

By asking these questions, I might get answers like this:

'Perhaps she got held back at work and really wanted to get home on time'; or 'Maybe she had to stop and help someone else'; or 'Something's come up that she just couldn't avoid'; or 'She had an accident on the way home'; or 'She just forgot because she's so busy at work'.

This thinking changes how I feel about the situation and interrupts the negative pattern that I created myself. The goal is to balance negative meanings with positive meanings and not be caught putting yourself in an un-resourceful state for absolutely zero reason.

You know what, even if something isn't true, when you give it a negative meaning you feel it and you experience sensations like it actually is true, like it's really happening.

You suffer the same range of negative emotions as if the situation were real.

Why would a sane person do that? Why not take control of how you feel so you avoid unnecessary pain and avoid damaging your relationships.

*'If you judge people, you have no time to love them.'*

**Mother Teresa of Calcutta**
**Yugoslav-born Missionary and Humanitarian**

## Ending Your Day

What about the end of your day? Do you ever go to bed feeling drained or empty or even frustrated about something? What if you ended your day by asking yourself questions like these:

- 'What is the best thing about my life?'

- 'What am I really thankful for?'

- 'If I were thankful for something in my life, what would it be?'

- 'Why am I thankful for that?'

- 'What's one solid lesson I can take away from today that makes me a better person?'

How would that affect you? How would that affect the quality of your emotions? How would you feel as you drift off to sleep?

I guess the best way to find out would be to try it.

The second type of question is probably the most basic type.

## 2. Focusing On Solutions and Options

Problems, problems, problems, we all have them. In fact, they are an essential element of life; they are a sign of life. The only people without problems are in a cemetery. The size of our problems is not the issue. Rather, it is whether or not we do something about them. The way we respond to the problems or challenges we experience in life shapes our character.

Any question that helps you to identify ways of dealing with a challenge and to explore many options leads you down the path of progress. Questions that fit in this category sound like 'What can I do to solve this?', 'What are five possible ways of dealing with this?' or 'Who else, from whom I can learn, has done this?'

The next question type is that which helps us to get the results we really want.

## 3. Taking Action

Questions that help change how you feel about doing something and actually get you to take the action you know you should take are tremendously empowering. Questions like,

- 'What must I do right now to get the result I want?' or

- 'How can I make this happen?' or

- 'Why must I do this right now?' …..

…. shift your focus away from procrastination to action.

Our behaviour is guided by a simple law which I refer to as the 'law of dominant behaviour'. I actually think I'm the originator of that term.

## BE THE VOICE

*When two opposing behaviours are an option, the one with which we associate the least pain or the most pleasure will dominate.*

To motivate ourselves to take action, all we have to do is change the emotion that we associate with the action. To do that we have to change our frame of reference from;

- doing it means effort and not doing it or doing something else instead means pleasure;

To this ..

- not doing it means we pay a price and doing it means pleasure or benefit of some kind.

By having this new perspective in mind, we are more likely to take the action we know we must take.

Any question that focuses the mind on why inaction is painful and action is beneficial fits into this category. Questions such as these:

- 'What will it cost me if I do not do this right now?'

- 'What price will I pay if I do nothing?'

- 'How will this benefit me in the long term?'

- 'What will I get by taking action now?'

Questions like these help move us away from inaction.

Now, I should point out that this might get us to start taking action; it does not mean we shall keep it going. How many people start an exercise program and eventually give it away? Why does that happen?

The answer is quite simple; anything that causes us pain cannot be sustained over the long term. The brain is wired to move us away from pain and towards pleasure, so if behaviour such as exercising is always associated with pain it will ultimately be discontinued. The person will never follow through. If the action brings us pleasure, it's more likely to be sustained.

Questions like these help you start the process of associating pleasure to the behaviours you want.

- 'How can I make doing this fun and enjoyable?'

- 'Where could I do this that's a more pleasant environment?' (I used this one when I wrote my first book, it was such a long and arduous process that changing the environment in which I wrote to coffee shops made the journey all that more pleasurable.)

- 'Who could do this with me and make it easier?'

- 'What's a more enjoyable way to achieve the outcome?'

All of these work.

The fourth question type is one that has the ability to make us really stand out from the crowd.

# 4. Taking Responsibility

What do I mean by 'taking responsibility'? In this context I mean taking ownership for doing something to change a situation instead of ignoring it or complaining about it.

I recently flew from Melbourne to Brisbane in Australia on an early morning flight. As we took off, I felt a tickle in my throat that caused me to break into a fit of coughing. I just couldn't get rid of the tickle.

I was sitting in row 1 in the aisle and one of the flight attendants was seated in a direct line of sight to where I was seated. When the seat belt lights went off, the flight attendants removed their seat belts and then moved into the galley area to set up for their usual flight routine. A short moment later, the flight attendant who could see me from her seat came over and gave me a glass of water, and also offered me a throat-soothing lozenge. She then gave me some advice about what I could to do reduce the coughing when I finally got home.

Now she was not obliged to do any of that. She could have continued with her routine and nothing would have been said. In fact, I probably would not even have noticed. But no, she took action based on the answers to questions like these; 'What can I do to help this person?' or 'How can I make this person's flight more comfortable?' Instead of ignoring me she took responsibility and as a result really differentiated herself, and her airline for that matter.

People who fail to take responsibility, and who prefer to leave it for others ask questions and make statements like these ... 'Why don't they do something about this?' or 'When will they do something about this?' or 'Nobody ever trains me'.

The reality of this type of internal conversation is that it will hold these people back from progress, certainly in their career. At the very best, it will cause them to stay right where they are in their work and in their personal life. They are noticed at work for all of the wrong reasons. They can never stand out as employees and the lack of progression in their organisation leads them to ask more questions; 'Why don't they appreciate me?' or 'Why can't I get promoted?'

People who really stand out from the crowd are those who take responsibility. They communicate to themselves in a different way and these types of questions dominate their thoughts:

- 'What can I do about this?'

- 'How can I help?'

- 'Whom can I get to help me on this?'

- 'What can I do to get them to move on this?'

## BE THE VOICE

- 'To whom can I speak in order to get action here?'

When you have a conversation like this with yourself, your focus shifts from what other people can do and should do, to what you can do. Then you stand out from the crowd.

In the appendices you'll find a toolkit of questions, questions that you can ask in a range of situations. My intention here is to give you the foundations for really mastering this concept.

> *'At the judgement day a man will be called upon to account for all the good things he might have enjoyed and did not enjoy.'*
>
> **Jewish Proverb**

# Final Thoughts

While this book is not quite finished at this point, I felt it was appropriate to partially conclude it here.

While I've listed many questions in the appendices you might use in different circumstances, my intent was not that you learn those questions specifically. Rather, I wanted you to understand the concept of taking control of your mind and the conversation that goes on within, taking control of how you feel on a consistent basis and ultimately take control of the way you experience life.

My hope is that you now decide to master this communication skill and through constant and conscious application make it a conditioned pattern of behaviour. If you do that, I know the quality of your life will move in a positive direction. Your ability and character as an employee, as a leader, as a friend, as a parent and as a partner will grow and you will find yourself even more influential in shaping the lives of others.

I often say to people that one of our most important roles we perform as a human being is to influence the way others experience life. Think about it, as a parent you help shape the life of a child, as a husband or wife you help shape the life of your partner, as a member of society you help shape the lives of people you interact with.

However, remember this:

> *You can only shape the life of others to the extent you can shape your own; you can only communicate with others to the level that you can communicate with yourself. Mastery of self precedes mastery of others!*

Armed with the skills of life mastery, such as the ability to ask great questions, you *can* take your life to the next level and shape it in such a way that others want to learn from you.

BE THE VOICE

# The Resources Are There Already

We often forget that some of the most powerful tools and resources for changing the quality of our lives already reside within us. We are all led to believe that by having things or buying things we get what we want emotionally. We associate pleasure with the products we are offered through the constant bombardment and conditioning of advertising. You know what I am talking about here.

We get to experience joy when we buy a new phone. We become an adventurer when we buy a chicken burger. We get wings when we drink a certain drink. We get to wind down and experience a sense of peace when we drink that special cup of coffee... these are the types of associations that people create.

Truth is the feelings of joy and fulfilment are created internally, not by the things we have, not by the events in our life. The first step in really taking control of the quality of your life starts with taking control of your mind through your internal conversation, through asking great questions.

Imagine what it would be like if you could have all the nice things and be consistently fulfilled in every area of your life. Imagine what it would be like to have relationships that are extraordinary. Imagine accelerating your career to a new level. Imagine being a leader that even more people admire and want to follow. How would you like that? What would your life be like if you could change the way you feel at any moment?

Let me tell you, the quality of your life would change because the quality of your life is the quality of the emotions you consistently engage in. I hope in some small way I've contributed to these outcomes becoming a reality for you.

*'Nothing ever becomes real till it is experienced. Even a proverb is no proverb to you till your life has illustrated it.'*

**John Keats (1795 - 1821) - English Poet**

# The First Responder Paradox

I began this book with a story about a selection course for special operations. Selection programs of this nature are designed to sort the chaff from the wheat. They do that by pushing candidates to their physical limits. When they hit those limits the selectors get to see and remove those who do not actually have the physical capacity to do the job, and those who do have the capacity but run shitty conversations inside their own heads and then act in accordance with those inner conversations.

I've seen people give up when they had more to give. I've also experienced those moments when your inner voice says you need to stop, you need to rest, you even start to justify why it's ok to stop and what you'll say to people when you do.

I've also learnt that you can push on if you take control of that inner voice and change the conversation. What worked for me was telling myself "these pussies will never break me". Did it hurt to push on, sure did. Did it feel good to not give up, absolutely. Call it ego, call it what you like, but the idea of being one of the few never failed to keep me going.

The people who run these selection programs simply choose those people who obviously control their inner voice when pushing beyond the normal physical limitations, those who don't give up when physical output is required, regardless of what's left in the fuel tank.

But here's what I believe is the first responder paradox.

Many of those who get through those selection courses, control the voice in their head in one area of life, that area being when physical achievement is required. As long as the external stimulus requires a physical commitment, they have that pattern embedded deeply in their psyche.

But when the need for physical achievement is gone, maybe they leave the unit or they retire, they often lose the source of motivation to control how they think.

Many fall back to the norm and let the inner voice run its own patterns, uncontrolled, especially when dealing with the only real challenges they're now confronted with - mental challenges associated with events of the past and present.

I have a deep respect for not only my special operations brothers and sisters, but they/we are not the only ones affected by this.

Our fellow first responders and defence personnel are also affected; this book is dedicated to you all.

You have been repeatedly exposed to some of the worst things a human can be exposed to. If you simply forgot, if your memory was erased, any negative feelings or associations you have with those events would simply vanish and life would proceed without any ill effects.

But it doesn't work out that way, does it?

## You Have A Choice

The memories remain, so that leaves you with a choice. A choice of how you think about and respond emotionally to those events. And those who know me know I say this from personal experience.

This is what I suggest:

First, STOP posting annually about the tragedies of the past and everything that happened to you and others. Let history remain in the past. When you focus on it now, it becomes the present.

For more details and information about studies on this specific topic, and why revisiting the past annually can and does have negative results, refer to the notes in Appendix A.

Second, ask yourself better questions so the meaning of those events is eventually turned from a pure tragedy to something with more balance.

What did you learn from those events that made you a better person? How has that event made you stronger? How did those events make you a person better able to coach and support others? Why are you a better parent because of those events? What lessons can you take from those events that allows you to help others exposed to the same thing?

I truly hope you're getting this.

You owe it to yourself, and to those who might have lost their life or made sacrifices in the past to do that.

# Man's Search for Meaning

One final story about a book I read many years ago, written by Victor E Frankl. It was titled 'Man's Search for Meaning'.

In this book, Frankl, a psychiatrist and Holocaust survivor, shares his harrowing experiences in Nazi concentration camps and the psychological insights he drew from them.

At the heart of Frankl's philosophy is the idea that while we cannot always control what happens to us, we can control how we respond.

He observed that those who survived the camps were often those who could find meaning, even in suffering.

Frankl's central message is deeply empowering: between stimulus and response, there is a space, and in that space lies our power to choose. That choice shapes our growth and our freedom. His development of logotherapy - a therapeutic approach centred on the human drive to find meaning - offers a path to reclaim agency, even in the most oppressive circumstances.

As a complement to the themes of this book, Frankl's work affirms the transformative power of the inner voice. By learning to reinterpret past events through a lens of meaning rather than pain, we can reshape our

## BE THE VOICE

emotional landscape. We are not victims of our past—we are the authors of the story we tell ourselves about it.

> *"It is a powerful mind that can take what seems to be a tragedy, extract the value from it and turn it into more than a waste of life."*

# Appendices

## A: Revisiting Past Tragedies, When You Should and Shouldn't

I've been solid in staying away from revisits to past events unless it is meaningful to myself or others. If it's to give honour to someone, or to help others, or to do as we are doing here which is to teach a value adding skill; it makes sense to me to go back to those events.

Other than that, I stay away, I let sleeping dogs lie.

I forget why this took place or what specifically prompted it, but this is a topic I've studied in detail over the past decade. I went down the rabbit hole, and like my buddy Adam would say, was down that hole rummaging around with a torch, trying to find answers.

Here's what I know.

### Why Reposting Past Tragedies Might Be Hurting More Than Helping

Each year, many people post on social media to mark the anniversary of a personal or public tragedy. For some, it's a way to honour loved ones or acknowledge a painful chapter in their lives. But while the intention is often heartfelt, research suggests that repeatedly reliving and sharing past traumas, especially online, might be doing more harm than good, both for the person posting and for those who see it.

### It's Like Reopening a Wound

When we revisit a traumatic event, especially through images, videos, or emotional writing, it can feel like we're right back there emotionally. In fact, a study on the Boston Marathon bombings showed something surprising: people who watched a lot of media coverage of the event reported higher levels of stress than some of the people who were actually there (Holman, Garfin, & Silver, 2014).

In other words, seeing or posting about trauma again and again can reinforce those painful feelings, instead of helping us move on.

I think it was Tony Robbins who said *"The past does not become your future unless you live there."*

## Talking Isn't Always Healing—It Can Be Rumination

There's a difference between processing a difficult experience and getting stuck in it. Psychologist Susan Nolen-Hoeksema spent years studying something called rumination, which is what happens when we replay negative events in our minds without reaching any resolution.

Her research showed that people who ruminate are more likely to feel depressed and anxious over time (Nolen-Hoeksema et al., 2008).

Reposting sad or traumatic content every year might seem like a way to cope, but if it's just repeating the same pain without progress, it could be keeping us stuck where we are.

## Our Feelings Are Contagious, Especially Online

Social media doesn't just share information, it spreads emotion. A fascinating study by Facebook researchers found that people's emotions could actually "rub off" on others through social networks. If you're exposed to a lot of negative or sad content, you're more likely to feel that way too, even if you don't realise it (Kramer, Guillory, & Hancock, 2014).

So when we repeatedly post about painful experiences, we may unintentionally be passing on distress to others, especially those who are vulnerable or have gone through similar things.

## When Tragedy Becomes Identity

Sometimes a major life event like the loss of a loved one, a disaster, or personal trauma, can start to define who we are. Psychologists call this "trauma centrality", meaning the event becomes a central part of someone's identity (Berntsen & Rubin, 2006).

While finding meaning in suffering is important, being too tightly bound to a tragic story can make it hard to grow beyond it. If the same story is revisited every year in the same way, it may reflect that we haven't fully integrated it into our life's journey.

Identity was always an issue for my sister. She used to say to me "I am depressed" ... and get annoyed with me when I would correct her with "you mean you're feeling depressed." She always resisted; for her it was how she identified herself.

## Social Media Isn't Therapy

While it's natural to want to share what we're feeling, it's worth remembering that social media is not designed for emotional processing. It's often not a safe or supportive environment, and emotional posts can attract silence, shallow reactions, or even unhelpful comments. That can leave people feeling misunderstood or worse; more alone. What looks like connection can sometimes backfire emotionally.

I know personally I see repeated posts from old work mates about tragic events. I also see comments on those posts from people that are well intended, but unintentionally reinforce all of the negativity around the event and feelings of sorrow. I say nothing, I read and remain silent not wanting to reinforce anything or give attention to someone because they are sad. In those moments I actually don't know what to say that would help. My comments would probably be perceived as cold or uncaring.

## A Healthier Way to Remember

None of this means we should forget or suppress our painful experiences. Honouring the past is part of being human. But we might want to ask ourselves: "Am I sharing this to heal, or to relive the pain?" If it's the latter, it may be worth exploring different ways to remember like having a private moment, creating something meaningful, or talking with someone who can really listen.

In the end, growth never comes from repeating the same story over and over again, it can only come from writing the next chapter.

## References

Given the nature of this section, I think it's important to highlight references for some of these ideas.

1. Holman, E. A., Garfin, D. R., & Silver, R. C. (2014). Media's role in risk and resilience following the Boston Marathon bombings. Proceedings of the National Academy of Sciences, 111(1), 93–98. https://doi.org/10.1073/pnas.1316265110

2. Nolen-Hoeksema, S., Wisco, B. E., & Lyubomirsky, S. (2008). Rethinking Rumination. Perspectives on Psychological Science, 3(5), 400–424. https://doi.org/10.1111/j.1745-6924.2008.00088.x

3. Kramer, A. D. I., Guillory, J. E., & Hancock, J. T. (2014). Experimental evidence of massive-scale emotional contagion through social networks. Proceedings of the National Academy of Sciences, 111(24), 8788–8790. https://doi.org/10.1073/pnas.1320040111

4. Berntsen, D., & Rubin, D. C. (2006). The centrality of event scale: A measure of integrating a trauma into one's identity and its relation to post-traumatic stress disorder symptoms. Behaviour Research and Therapy, 44(2), 219–231. https://doi.org/10.1016/j.brat.2005.01.009

# B: Question Based Conversational Tools

*'To lead an extraordinary life, do the everyday common things in a way that is not common to others. To experience the joy that life offers regardless of circumstance, think in a way that is not common to others.'*

In this section I have provided you with a range of questions you can use during internal and also external conversation, to empower yourself and/or people around you. They are grouped into different contexts I believe would be common for most people.

## 1. Change How You Feel About a Past Experience or Loss

We all have experiences in our life that we would prefer not to have had. However, that being the case, we have to face the fact that the one thing we cannot control or influence in any way is our past. It's happened and cannot be undone. However, what we can control is how we feel about the experience.

To change how we feel about an experience, all we need to do is change the meaning we give to the experience. To do that we simply change what we focus on.

Questions like these change your focus, stop you from ignoring the positives of an experience you were exposed to, and turn it into something from which you can extract some sort of value.

- 'How can I use this experience in a positive way?'

- 'How will this serve me in the future?'

- 'What can I learn from this that prepares me better for the future?'

- 'How does this experience help me grow as a person?'

- 'What's funny about this?'

- 'How will this experience ultimately shape me and make me stronger as a person?'

- 'How does having this experience make it easier for me to help others?'

- 'How can I contribute to others even more because of this experience?'

> *'The past is no more than a memory that lives on the path to my present consequences. It has power over me only to the extent that I give it power. I can choose to move freely away and release it for I am not my past, I am my future.'*

Some experiences are more that just exposure to a terrible or tragic event, they can involve actual personal loss. I believe these are in many ways more difficult to deal with than exposure to events without that type of loss.

Limiting this to a loss associated with a loved one or some person you were connected to, here's some questions to consider and adapt.

- 'What advice would [the person] give me if we could speak right now?'

- 'What would [the person] be most thankful for in regard to our relationship?'

- 'What learnings can I take from [the person] / [or the event] that at least give the situation [or event] some value?'

- 'What did I do that [the person] would be most thankful for?'

- 'How has my relationship with [the person] made me a better or stronger person?'

- 'What are the positive or at least neutral details that I'm not considering here?'

## 2. Change How You Feel About Your Current Situation

You can also change how you feel about a present experience. Let me offer you two slightly different approaches in this regard.

## Change Meaning

The first approach is to change what the situation means to you. The meaning you give to the experience or situation can be changed by using the questions mentioned in the preceding section.

## Contrast

One of the simplest and most effective ways to change how you feel about a situation is to contrast it to one you perceive to be less desirable. For example, if I am down to my last 100 dollars, I guess I could feel lousy about my situation. However, if I take a moment to reflect on those people who have not even that much money, I can change my emotional state.

Some years ago I had a conversation with a friend who owned a coffee shop at the shopping centre close to where we lived. She was hobbling about with a bulging disk in her back, finding it very hard to move and virtually impossible to stay on her feet all day. I asked her how she was dealing with it and she told me that she had been feeling very sorry for herself until a guy in a wheelchair rolled past her earlier that morning. The first thought that she had was, 'At least I'm not in a wheelchair'. As that thought crossed her mind, she made a judgment about her present situation from a completely different frame of reference. And as a result felt different about it. The pain was not relieved, but her attitude and emotional state changed instantly.

What she had done was contrast her situation to one less desirable to her, and as a result had a different basis from which to determine how she felt about her situation.

Parents use this approach frequently. For example, when a child asks for a designer pair of jeans and the parents remind them of the children who never get to buy any clothes and wear only what they receive from charity, they are using contrast to change behaviour.

If confronted by a problem or challenge or your current situation that seems to get you down and puts you in a less than resourceful state, you can use the power of contrasting by asking questions like these.

## BE THE VOICE

- 'How could this be worse?'

- 'What would be a worse situation than this?'

- 'Who is in a much worse position than I am?'

- 'For what am I thankful for in this situation?'

- 'If I could be thankful for something in this situation, what would it be?'

- 'What's actually good about this situation?'

The only problem with contrasting is that it can work against you if you let it. Let me give you an example to explain what I mean.

Let's say you are unhappy with your current physical state. Suppose you are extremely overweight and that is a source of distress for you. You wanted to change but find it difficult. You could contrast against someone in a far worse situation and realise that your situation was not so bad. If that causes you to settle for the current situation and not take any action about changing it, contrasting has not served you. In fact it's done exactly the opposite and held you back from making change. It's actually caused you to settle for a situation that is undesirable.

That is not the intention of contrasting. The intention is to change the way you feel about the current situation so that you put yourself in a resourceful state that helps you effectively deal with the situation. You are more likely to tap into the resources you have from this state as opposed to a negative emotional state.

> *'We spend so much time yearning for that special item that will finally make us happy, that we don't take the time to look around and discover that we already are.'*
>
> **Anonymous**

## 3. Get Yourself To Take Action And Follow Through

To get ourselves to take action, all we have to do is change what we associate with the action. To do that we have to change our frame of reference to;

    a. Not doing it means we pay a price; and

    b. Doing it means pleasure or benefit of some kind.

To achieve this, ask questions from this list.

- 'If I don't do this, how will that hurt me?'

- 'What are the consequences for me if I don't do this?'

- 'By not doing this, what price will I ultimately pay?'

- 'If I don't start doing this right now, what will my situation be in five years?'

- 'If I do this what benefits will it bring?'

- 'By doing this, how does that benefit me?'

- 'What will I gain by doing this?'

Sometimes we need to acknowledge that we are taking action that holds us back.

    'What is this action, that's holding me back and that I must stop doing?'

Starting to take action and following through over the long term are two entirely different things. Discipline will get you started, but on its own it is not enough. The only way any action will last is if it becomes pleasurable in some way.

You can start the process of associating pleasure to the behaviours you want by asking these questions.

- 'How can I make doing this fun and enjoyable?'

- 'Where could I do this to make it more enjoyable?'

- 'How could I make this more exciting or add variety into it?'

- 'Who could I do this with to make it easier to do?'

- 'Is there another way that I can achieve this that would be more enjoyable?'

- 'What could I do to make it a growing experience while I do it?'

> *'There are risks and costs to a program of action, but they are far less than the long-term risks and costs of comfortable inaction.'*
>
> **John F. Kennedy (1917 - 1963) - US President 1960 - 1963**

## 4. Solve Problems Or Deal With Challenges

We all have problems or challenges in our life. In fact they are a sign of life. Questions like these help you deal with and solve problems.

- 'What can I do right now about this?'

- 'What are ten (or however many) ways I could potentially solve this?'

- 'What must I do to solve this?'

- 'Who can help me solve this?'

- 'Who has solved a similar problem, from whom I can learn,?'

- 'What similar problems have I dealt with in the past that give me clues for ways to deal with this?'

*'He knows not his own strength that hath not met adversity.'*
**Ben Jonson (1573 - 1637) - English dramatist**

## 5. Change Beliefs About What You Can Do And Achieve

Have you ever said, 'I couldn't do that' or 'I don't have the time' or 'I don't have the education for that' or 'I'm just not smart enough to do that'? Have you ever made a statement like this as an indication of some belief you have that would ultimately stop you from doing or attempting to do something? My illusion is that you probably have. I think we have all done it at some time.

These are just statements that communicate a belief we hold. It does not mean they are true and in most cases they are false. The sad truth is that when we hold these types of beliefs, we take action aligned to them. Accordingly, we get results that reinforce these beliefs. When we believe that we can do something or that, if we just commit ourselves, we can achieve anything, we tend to take different action and the great results we get reinforce these beliefs.

If you find yourself saying these things to yourself, or even aloud, these questions might help you develop a set of beliefs that serve you instead of holding you back. These questions focus your mind on what you have achieved and what others have achieved, a tremendous source of belief.

- 'How does holding these beliefs prevent me from getting the results I want?'

- 'If I don't change what I believe, what will that cost me (now, in two years time, in five years time)?'

- 'What challenges have I dealt with in the past that I thought I would never get through at the time?'

- 'What have I achieved that I once thought impossible?'

- 'When have I taken action in the past and ultimately got the results I set out to achieve, even though I did not know how at the start?'

- 'Who has solved problems or dealt with challenges even more difficult than this one?'

- 'Who has made a remarkable achievement that most people would have thought impossible?'

- 'What beliefs must I have about myself to deal with this?'

- 'What evidence have I got that shows I can do this if I just take action?'

- 'If I *could* do this, what *would* I do?'

*'Whether you believe you can do a thing or believe you can't, you are right.'*

**Henry Ford (1863 – 1947)**
**American Motor Vehicle Manufacturer**

## 6. Continually Improve

Change is a constant. It is an inevitable process that none of us can avoid. Our choice is not whether or not we want to change, but rather which direction we want the change to take – improvement or decline. Endless commitment to continual improvement is the discipline of success in life. Questions like these are the tools of that discipline.

- 'How can I make this better?'

- 'What's another (or a better) way of doing this?'

- 'What else could I do to make this better?'

- 'What could I do to make this more pleasurable to undertake?'

- 'Who can I learn from?'

- 'If I was being personally coached by (someone you admire), what would they tell me to do differently?'

## 7. Stand Out From The Crowd

Do you want to know how to become an outstanding employee, an outstanding leader, someone that really stands out in any organisation? Think beyond your job description, walk that extra mile, do what needs to be done because it is the right thing to do, not because your job description says you have to do it.

Ask yourself questions like these.

- 'What can I do?'

- 'How can I help?'

- 'What needs to be done to fix this?'

- 'What can I do for this person?'

- 'How can I make this better?'

- 'What must I do right now to make this better?'

You should notice that these questions have three common elements.

1. They are started with the words what or how;

2. They contain the word 'I'; and

3. They end with some action based word or phrase.

Combine these three elements into your questions and you become personally responsible. When you do that you will stand out even more.

BE THE VOICE

*'After all is said and done, more is said than done.'*

**Anonymous**

# 8. Create Extraordinary Relationships

I believe that these are the most important questions you can ever bring to any relationship.

- 'What meaning have I given to this situation?'

- 'Do I have all of the information I need to be able to give this its true meaning?'

- 'Is it possible I am wrong?'

- 'What other meaning could this situation really have?'

By asking any one of these questions, you open your mind to the possibility that some behaviour you dislike in another person might not mean what you think. You discard the illusion that the behaviour is about you and start to recognise that you do not really know.

Other questions that can help you take your relationship to an extraordinary level include these.

- 'What do I love most about (my partner)?'

- 'What could I say to (my partner) that would make (her or him) realise that I will always be here for (her or him)?'

- 'What can I do for (my partner) that would make (her or him) feel needed or important?'

- 'What could I say to (my partner) that would make (her or him) feel needed or important?'

- 'What am I thankful for in this relationship?'

- 'What could I do to really surprise (my partner)?'

- 'What could I do that would make this relationship more exciting for both of us?'

- 'What could I do to make (my partner's) day?'

- 'What could I do to show (my partner) that I really love (her or him)?'

- 'What could I say to (my partner) that would make (her or him) really feel loved by me?'

- 'How could I convey my love for (my partner) without actually saying anything?'

> *'The world is a looking glass, and gives back to every man the reflection of his own face.'*
>
> **William Makepeace Thackeray (1811 - 1863)**
> **English Writer**

## 9. Deal With Unhappy Customers

How do you feel when you have to serve a customer who is unhappy or cranky? Some people say it depends on how many of them I have to serve in a day. I guess that is true. How do you deal with those customers? Do you get cranky back at them or do you just treat them with contempt? Do you make some judgment about the type of person they are and, as a result, treat them in a way that might cause them not to come back?

Remember this. People do things for positive intent. Customers do not set out to make you unhappy or angry, or come into your shop or office with the intent of hurting you. They do what they need to do to meet their own needs and when they are unhappy or cranky then something is probably happening in their life that you do not know about. Their needs are not being met in some specific area of their life. Try asking yourself questions like these.

- 'What might be happening in their life that I don't know about that would cause them to be this way?'

- 'If I were feeling that way, what would it take to cheer me up while being served?'

- 'What could I do right now to make their day a little better?'

- 'By making this customer's day just a little better when nobody else takes the time, what sort of person do I become (or how does that serve the business)?'

If you ask those questions, how would that change your behaviour towards them? How would this behaviour affect your business? Let me tell you, when you deal with unpleasant customers from this frame of mind, you differentiate yourself and your business.

*'A man's feeling of good-will towards others is the strongest magnet for drawing good-will towards himself.'*

**Lord Chesterfield (1694 - 1773)**
**English statesman**

## 10. Start And Plan Your Day

Most people in business start their day with a 'to do' list. Do you ever get through it? Do you ever feel yourself getting stressed during the day as you try to complete as many of these tasks as you can with the constant interruptions? If you want to change the quality of your life on a daily basis, shift your focus away from 'to do' lists to getting specific results or outcomes in areas of your personal and business life that are important to you.

- 'What outcomes or results am I committed to achieving today?'

## BE THE VOICE

- 'Why are those outcomes important to me?'

- 'Why are they important to the business?'

- 'What must I do to achieve those outcomes?'

- 'What am I going to do today to move closer to my own goals?'

- 'What can I do today to help _____ move closer to their goals?'

- 'Who could help me do these things so I'm not lumbered with everything?'

BE THE VOICE

*'The time to repair the roof is when the sun is shining.'*
**John F. Kennedy (1917 – 1963)
President of the United States**

## 11. Avoid Getting Somebody Else's Useless To Do List

Do people ever come to you to get you to do something for them at work? Of course they do, everybody does it at some time. There is nothing really wrong with that if the task is to achieve an important outcome and there is no better way to do it. To make sure these criteria are met and reduce the likelihood that you end up with someone else's 'to do' list, ask those people these questions.

- 'What outcome are you trying to achieve?'

- 'Why is that important to you or the business?'

- 'What might be a better way of achieving this?'

- 'When do you really need to have it done by?'

When you ask questions like these, you become a coach to others. You're teaching them to think about results and the importance of those results as opposed to activities, and to focus only on the 'must dos' in getting those results. You start to pull them away from just writing 'to do' lists.

*'Time is what we want most, but what, alas, we use worst.'*
**William Penn (1644 - 1718)
English Quaker and Founder of Pennsylvania, USA**

## 12. End The Day Positively

Why not end your day in a positive state and ask yourself questions like these?

- 'What did I learn today?'

- 'How can I use what I have learnt?'

- 'On a scale of 1 to 10, how much did I enjoy today?'

- 'What can I do to make tomorrow even more enjoyable?'

- 'What can I do to make (insert a specific activity) more enjoyable to do?'

- 'What did I achieve today?'

- 'What's not working and that I have to change?'

- 'What's good about my life?'

- 'For what am I really thankful in my life?'

- 'Why am I thankful for that?'

- 'If I were going to be thankful for something in my life, what would it be?'

Questions empower not only you but they can also be used to empower and positively influence people around you.

*'Study the past, if you would divine the future.'*
**Confucius (551 – 479 BC) - Chinese philosopher**

## 13. Change How Someone Else Feels

Have you ever tried to get someone who is unhappy to change his or her state? How do you usually do that? My experience is that most people tell others to be happy. For example, your friend or one of your children is unhappy for no apparent reason. You say something like, 'Come on, it can't be that bad, put it out of your mind and smile'. The problem with this approach is that it does not interrupt their thinking pattern at that time.

## BE THE VOICE

They are thinking in a particular way, focusing on the negative aspects of something and adopting the psychology of someone who is unhappy.

Let me suggest a more effective way that is very useful for parents with children. In the first instance you have to interrupt their pattern of thinking. Here are some ideas.

- Ask, 'What would it take to get you to eat a mud pie?'

- Tell them 'Because of the economic situation, we are going to have to let one of you go'.

- Put on a ballet tutu or a set of Mickey Mouse ears.

- Push your hair up into a Mohawk style.

- Skip to the bathroom.

- Put your shirt on back the front.

Okay, you get the idea. My point is that you should do something or ask something that interrupts their thinking pattern. Once you have done that, you can ask questions that help direct their focus elsewhere.

- 'What's been good about your day?'

- 'What can you do to make your day better?'

- 'What do you love?'

- 'What are you good at?'

- 'If this were your last day on earth (or at school), what would you love to do?'

You can also ask questions that help them change what an experience means to them as we have already discussed.

## 14. Prepare Someone For Learning

This is one for you trainers. Many people go to seminars or training programs. However, most do not think about specifically what they want to get out of it. At your opening, you can have people take responsibility for taking something out of the program by asking these questions and having them to write the answers in their notes.

- 'Why are you here (on this course)?

- 'What do you want to get out of this program (or course)?'

- 'Why is that important to you?'

- 'What must *you* do to get that outcome (those outcomes)?'

> *'What we have to learn to do, we learn by doing.'*
>
> **Aristotle (384 – 322 BC)**
> **Greek philosopher**

## 15. Change Someone's Behaviour

The basis for changing someone's behaviour is simply changing what they associate with the old behaviour and the desired behaviour. By asking questions like these you can start the process of changing their associations. I say start because it doesn't mean it will be sustained over time.

- 'What will it cost you if you continue that behaviour?'

- 'How is that behaviour ultimately going to hurt you?'

- 'If you continue this behaviour, what price are you eventually going to pay?'

- 'By performing (the new behaviour), how will you benefit in the long term?'

- 'By performing (the new behaviour), how will others benefit?'

- 'How will (the new behaviour) benefit you? '

Remember this. To tell is to do what is comfortable, to ask is an art form that few take the time to master.

## 16. Help Someone Learn From An Experience

Every experience, whether a formal training activity or just a life experience, offers learning opportunities. Asking quality questions, like these that follow, is the means for exploiting these opportunities.

- 'What did you learn from this experience?'

- 'How can you use what you've learned in the future (or at work)?'

- 'What challenges did you overcome?'

- 'How did you overcome those challenges?'

- 'What, specifically, worked for you?'

- 'If you did it again, what would you do differently?'

- 'How does this apply to your work?'

- 'How can you use this in your job?'

- 'How can you use this in your personal life?'

- 'How is this better than what you've done in the past?'

- 'What are some examples of where you might have used this approach in the past to get a better outcome?'

- 'Where have you seen a similar approach?'

- 'How has this approach served them?'

## BE THE VOICE

- 'How is this like what people do at work?'

- 'If you were going to coach someone on this, what three tips would you give them to help them do it well?'

*'The questions we ask of ourselves have a profound impact on how we experience life and what we are able to get ourselves to do. By using questions to direct our minds with precision, we can really tap into the power and resources we hold within.'*

# About the Author

George Lee Sye's fascination with human behaviour and the mind started in the mid 1980s. Intent on understanding how to accelerate the process of building connection and rapport with people in his work, he began a journey of discovery that has now influenced every aspect of his life, both personal and professional.

After involvement in a high risk job where a shotgun was accidentally fired by a team member behind him during a forced entry into a target building, George went on a deep dive study into why a routine well practiced behaviour [entering a building forcefully and exercising good weapon control] would change when emotions were altered by circumstances. What he learnt about the emotional layer of activity forever changed how he trained people in those roles and also in public speaking.

Through his seminars, personal coaching, and books, George has devoted himself to passing on his knowledge and skill for creating a remarkable quality of life. What he's learnt through reading, trial and error and an incredible diversity of experiences is now the foundation for positively impacting the lives of literally thousands of people.

George writes like he talks. He's not an academic, he's a practical man with a fairly simple mind. His goal has always been to communicate to people in simple and practical terms using life examples that people can relate to. His success in this area has come predominantly through his belief that delivering an idea without a way of using it is nothing more than giving people another topic of conversation. Unless the idea converts to some form of action or behavioural change that positively affects a one's life, it's a waste of time.

His ability to simplify what are often considered to be complex topics is remarkable. As a result, he has been able to create considerable value for companies with whom he's worked in the area of business improvement, and his popularity as a corporate educator, speaker and personal coach has grown consistently.

For more information about George and his work, visit his personal website and his professional training platform.

georgeleesye.com

9skillsfactory.com/accelerate

# Acknowledgements

As I reflect on my life so far, I realise I was not born thinking this way. Rather, the influence of some special people has helped shape me in many ways, and to these I will be forever grateful.

To Bob Atkinson (Commissioner of Police) and Bob Watson; thank you both for consistently asking great questions of me and challenging my thinking during some of the most exciting and interesting years of my life.

To Ivan 'Magpie' Brodie; a man who showed every person he came into contact with during his time in this world that happiness is really created within. I had the opportunity to catch up with Magpie a week before he died, but I didn't take it. I regret that decision to this day. RIP my friend.

To the remarkable men and women I worked with in SERT, your character, problem solving readiness and resilience stands out from the norm and has influenced me forever.

To my kids; Nicky and Matt, you'll probably never know how much being around you has helped me grow and how much love you've brought into my life.

To the women who have positively impacted my life, Debbie and Vicki, deep feelings of gratitude for your support will never wane.

Finally, I am thankful to the amazing men and women I work with at the California Superbike School, for you have continued my development by challenging and enhancing how I think about many things in both my personal and professional life.

BE THE VOICE

# Companion Read: Problem Warrior

If Be the Voice is about mastering the inner conversation that shapes how you feel about your life, then *Problem Warrior* is about what you do when life pushes back.

The two books are designed to work together.

Be the Voice focuses on the internal dialogue that runs beneath the surface of your thoughts. It explores how the stories you tell yourself about past events, present circumstances, and future possibilities influence your emotional state, your confidence, and your sense of control. When that internal voice is unmanaged, it can quietly undermine even the best intentions.

Problem Warrior picks up where that inner work meets reality. It is about facing challenges directly, regulating emotion under pressure, and taking deliberate action when problems arise. It provides practical principles for

## BE THE VOICE

thinking clearly, making decisions, and moving forward when situations are uncomfortable, complex, or demanding.

Every problem you encounter is filtered through your internal voice.

Every response you choose is influenced by it.

When the voice is aligned, disciplined, and constructive, the principles in Problem Warrior become far more powerful. When the principles of Problem Warrior are applied consistently, the work of Be the Voice is reinforced through real-world experience.

Together, they form a complete loop: inner mastery and outer execution.

If the ideas in Be the Voice resonate with you and you want to turn that inner clarity into confident action, Problem Warrior is the natural companion read.

Read them together and you build both sides of the equation: the voice that guides you, and the warrior who acts.

**Available Globally from Amazon.**

BE THE VOICE

## GEORGE LEE SYE

www.georgeleesye.com

9skillsfactory.com/accelerate

==========

www.ingramcontent.com/pod-product-compliance
Lightning Source LLC
Chambersburg PA
CBHW072201100426
42738CB00011BA/2496